MW00989639

"Dr. Chand's assignment in life is clearly to develop the church in unprecedented ways into what God has destined it to be at such a time as this."

Cynthia L. Hale,
Ray of Hope Christian Church, Decatur, Georgia

"Dr. Chand is an emerging voice in the arena of church leadership development. He challenges the church to be relevant and effective to the times. His voice is refreshing and thought provoking."

Tony Morris, Senior Leader,
New Covenant Christian Center, Seattle, Washington

WHO'S
HOLDING
YOUR
LADDER?

WHO'S HOLDING YOUR LADDER?

Leadership's Most Critical Decision – Selecting Your Leaders

SAMUEL R. CHAND
WITH CECIL MURPHEY

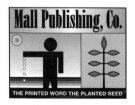

Niles, Illinois

Published by:
Mall Publishing Company
5731 West Howard Street
Niles, Illinois 60714
877.203.2453

Cover Design by Andrew Ostrowski

Book Design by Marlon B. Villadiego

ISBN 0-9741022-7-X

For licensing / copyright information, for additional copies
or for use in specialized settings contact:

Dr. Samuel R. Chand

Samuel R. Chand Ministries, Inc.
P.O. Box 18145
Atlanta, GA 30316

www.samchand.com or www.dreamreleaser.org
Email: samuel.chand@beulah.org

Table of Contents

1

Who's Holding Your Ladder?

I stared out the window while I waited for someone to call me into the sanctuary. I was a featured speaker at a conference at Evangel Church in Queens, New York. As I meditated on the points I wanted to cover, something in the street below diverted my attention.

A man stood on a ladder painting—not that uncommon a sight. I smiled, remembering my student days in Bible college. I had spent my summers doing that kind of work. Yet I couldn't take my eyes off the man. For several minutes I watched his graceful motions as he moved his brush across the surface.

"I wonder who's holding the ladder for him?" I asked aloud. I couldn't see all the way to the street level.

As I stood in pastor Robert Johansson's study, I kept thinking of that question. Someone had to be down there bracing the painter's ladder although I couldn't see him. My impression was made while I stared down from about eight floors above street level. As I watched the man paint the exterior wall, I noticed he could cover only a limited area. He stretched as far as he could to the left and then to the right and even reached above his head. As I observed him, it occurred to me that he was only going to the height that he was comfortable in climbing or reaching.

> **Whether in management or systems, the effectiveness of a leader depends on the person or persons who hold the ladder; those who are in support roles.**

What would allow him to go higher? I asked myself. I could see that he stood on an extension ladder, so he could go higher—and he would have to if he wanted to finish the job. If the ladder reached the top of the building, he still needed one thing. He had to have someone on the street level to hold his ladder steady while he worked.

By himself, the painter couldn't go any farther. He had stretched and reached and done everything he could by himself. He had to have help.

As I watched his graceful strokes I thought about that action in leadership terms. It struck me that, whether in management or systems, the effectiveness of a leader depends on the person or persons who hold the ladder—those who are in support roles.

Then another thought struck me: Those who hold the ladders are as important as the leaders themselves.

My mind wouldn't let go of that image. As I stared out that window in Queens, I kept thinking, no leader gets to the top without those down below who hold the ladder. I craned my neck trying to see the street level, but I never could see who held that ladder.

Then I smiled as my mind shifted to the symbolism of leadership, success, and people in enabling roles. Those who faithfully support from the bottom are often unseen. That doesn't diminish their importance or the need for them. It does mean that even though their ministries or their positions are every bit as important as the painter on the top, sometimes they do their work unnoticed. Sometimes God may be the only one who knows who's holding the ladder.

> *Sometimes God may be the only one who knows who's holding the ladder.*

I took the idea even further. I began to think of the ladder as the symbol of the dream—the vision of the leader—and, of course, that makes the painter the visionary. Once the visionaries start up their ladders, ministry can be large, and far-reaching, or narrow, and confined. The visionaries could have all the training possible, the most expensive equipment, years of experience and knowledge about painting, and could have all the expertise and be extremely passionate about what they're doing, but that's not the deciding factor. The ladder holder determines the height of the ladder climber. "That's it!" I cried out. "Those who hold the ladder control the ascent of the visionaries."

LADDERS AND LEADERSHIP

Long after I left the conference in Queens, I continued to dwell on that idea. I considered how that concept applies to leadership in business or in the church. Immediately, I remembered three examples (or paradigms as we like to call them today). I first heard them delivered as part of a powerful message by pastor Gerald Brooks from Grace Outreach Center in Plano, Texas. In a large conference I attended, he pointed out that there are three ways in which we do ministry.

The ladder holder determines the height of the ladder climber. Those who hold the ladder control the ascent of the visionaries.

The first is to do everything ourselves. That's how a number of leaders try to function, especially when the congregation is small. Eventually the realization hits: *That's too much work.*

The second is to hire it out. Some churches pay others to take over part or all of the load. *That's too much money.*

The third is to develop others. Some leaders teach people how to do the tasks. *That's too much time.*

Pastor Brooks pointed out that he had given us three paradigms and all of them had drawbacks. "What is the wise thing to do?" he asked.

Obviously, the answer is the third option—to develop others. However, too many church leaders get so busy painting at the top of their own ladders, they don't realize how much help they need. They don't realize the importance of developing ladder holders until they're sixty feet above ground and start to look down. Because they didn't teach others to hold the ladders for them, a few visionaries have fallen. Others have burned out from overwork and trying to do everything themselves. Some have simply quit trying. "It's just too hard," they say, "and too lonely."

Three ways in which we do ministry: The first is to do everything ourselves. That's too much work. The second is to hire it out. That's too much money. The third one is to develop others. That's too much time.

When I used the term *developing* others, I carefully chose that word instead of *training*. There is a vast difference between training people and developing them. Training focuses on tasks; developing focuses on the person. Training is uni-directional; developing is omni-directional. We train people to become receptionists. When we're finished, they're good receptionists and they do their tasks well. We have not developed them so that they are ready to move into other positions.

God never intended for the local church to be a one-person organization. That takes us back to the concept of developing leaders. If we don't develop and equip others, we're never going to have the kind of ladder holders we need—especially when we want to climb to the highest rungs.

Perhaps the best way to show how this works is to consider the contrast between *projects and people*. We leaders need ladder holders the most when we make the jump from activities to working with individuals. Projects involve policies, programs, buildings, ideas, or systems. Those are fairly stable and easily understood. We can usually control the variables.

When we move beyond projects, not only have we made a major leap, but we also have to change our way of thinking. We can't treat people the way we treat ideas or activities. Obviously, most people are egocentric and more concerned about themselves than with others. That is, they don't naturally care about serving God or others. That's something they have to learn in their growth process.

> *There is a vast difference between training people and developing them. Training focuses on tasks; developing focuses on the person.*

Realizing that fact about human nature forces us constantly to scramble for new answers. We need to help those we develop to:

- understand their purpose,
- grasp why their roles are important,
- cope with disappointment as well as with success,
- ignite their passion, be inspired to reach their fullest potential.

Some leaders feel as if they're progressing because action is going on. They point to the commotion and noise level around them. In reality, they may be going backward. Having many activities isn't always advancing. The proof comes when the tumult ceases. That's when people realize the action has been taking them backward.

We leaders need ladder holders the most when we make the jump from activities to working with individuals.

For example, this happens when leaders move from projects to people. Because they're not set up or taught to deal with people, they end up going back to the projects. That is, they end up managing rather than leading. We lead people, but we manage things.

Sometimes trying to move from projects to people ends in messy scandals, deep-seated anger, and serious recriminations. Many things are happening—even good things—but they don't extend the kingdom of God or enable Christians to grow.

Too many of those who call themselves leaders are actually good at projects. They can visualize what needs to be done. They are aware that unless the waters miraculously part, they'll need to build a bridge to take them across the Jordan River. They're often conscious of the need to get to the other side of the river while everyone else is enjoying the water. They grasp the problems involved in making a structure strong enough or wide enough. Too often, however, they don't know how to get it done because they don't know how to work well with people. They're aware only that they need a bridge built, and they can't understand why everyone doesn't volunteer and pitch in to accomplish the task. *They are project leaders.*

If they don't have excellent people skills, they focus on managing others—putting individuals into jobs to get the task completed. They have little concern for the talents or interests of those who are doing the task. "Just get it done," is the first sentence in their vocabulary.

This shows a crucial difference in leadership.

> **We lead people, but we manage things.**

Project leaders see the need, and we admire their concern to get things finished. They're not very concerned about who does what, so long as they get the bridge built and the ark of the covenant and all the priestly equipment get carried safely across the Jordan.

In short, dealing with projects is easier; dealing with people is more difficult.

By the time the project leaders set up camp on the east side of the Jordan, someone begins to realize that doing projects and building bridges aren't what really counts. They need bridges, of course, but they realize that the priorities are wrong. In the end, God's kingdom matures and stretches through people being edified, appreciated, and developed. In God's eyes, people count more than bridges, elevators, escalators, or ladders. All projects need people—but they need the right kind. They especially need the committed, talented workers to build the bridge correctly.

THE RIGHT LADDER HOLDERS

For days after I left Pastor Johansson's church, I thought about the ladder holders. I've been around thousands of leaders both in the marketplace and in ministry. I've come to one foundational understanding: The most important decision leaders make—no matter whether it's to build a bridge

Dealing with projects is easier; dealing with people is more difficult.

across the Jordan or erecting ladders to scale the walls of enemy strongholds—is to select the right helpers. If they don't have the right people holding the ladder, the project will fail.

In the church, we need to choose leaders who are involved, active, and already showing their commitment to Jesus Christ by their involvement. In business, we need the same kind of dedication. When we look at the qualities we seek, however, before anything else, we need to start with integrity.

Does that sound obvious? It may not be. I have a friend who became pastor of a church where they had a board of fifteen elders. Annually, the congregation elected five elders who served three years. That sounded fine, but the problem my friend faced was the election of those five elders each year.

He felt frustrated because most of the elders didn't attend Sunday school and yet they made decisions about the educational programs. Several of them didn't tithe, and yet they were the people who made decisions about church finances. Three of them attended church about once a month and spent more Sundays on the golf course than at worship, and yet they made the decisions about evangelism and outreach.

"Why did you elect him?" the pastor asked about one elder.

"To honor him. He's been in this church all his life and his daddy was an elder."

"He is one of the best businessmen in the city and people respect his decisions," said another. "He can help us make good decisions."

"If we make him an elder," was another response, "maybe he'll get active as a leader."

"Get him active as a leader," my friend countered, "and then make him an elder."

It took my pastor-friend two more years of the church electing elders for him to get across the need for integrity. It took another two years before he had a church board that functioned with vision and commitment. By the end of the fifth year of his ministry, he had people in leadership who faithfully worshiped every week and who gave at least ten percent of their income. Some taught Sunday school, sang in the choir, or participated in study groups. All of them had proven themselves in some form of ministry *before* they became elders. In short, they were people of integrity.

> *In God's eyes, people count more than bridges, elevators, escalators, or ladders.*

Why is this quality so crucial? The answer is that ultimately, the fulfillment of the vision depends on the people who support the ladder of the visionary leader.

Here's an example of how this works. I can change the light bulb in the ceiling in my living room. That's not a big problem because all I need is a six-foot stepladder. I can stand on whatever rung I need to reach the fixture. I don't need anyone to hold my ladder.

What happens if the bulbs on the outside that illuminate my driveway need changing (they are two stories up from the ground)? I can't change them from inside the house or by leaning down from the roof. The only way to get the bulbs changed is to use a twenty-foot ladder.

To stand twenty feet above the ground on a piece of wood eighteen inches by six is scary enough. What happens if the ladder begins to sway? What happens if I get up there and reach just an inch too far to the left? Yes, I need someone to hold my ladder.

A situation like that actually happened to me. One evening we had invited friends over to celebrate the birthday of our daughter, Rachel. She had turned eighteen. My wife Brenda had worked hard getting the house ready for guests. Earlier in the week she had given me a few outdoor chores to do, and one of them was to change the floodlights. I had forgotten to do that task.

> *The most important decision leaders make is to select the right helpers.*

Fifteen minutes before our first guests were due, I went to snap on the outside lights and they didn't come on. Then I remembered: I had forgotten to put in a new bulb.

"I'll get it done," I yelled as I raced into the garage,

grabbed a bulb, and pulled out my fold-up, handy dandy, Home Depot ladder. I set it up next to the garage. Then I turned around and looked at the distance from the ground. Until that moment, I hadn't realized how high the light was from the ground. I was experienced in climbing up and down ladders, so I shrugged. Just one bulb—no big deal—and I started climbing. About two-thirds of the way up, I felt the ladder begin to wobble—just a little— but enough that I knew it wasn't safe to keep going.

> *Ultimately, the fulfillment of the vision depends on the people who support the ladder of the visionary leader.*

"Rachel! Come and help," I called. "I need you to hold the ladder for me."

My daughter came outside and stared at me, not sure what she was supposed to do. She leaned forward with an arm on each side. I smiled at her naiveté.

"No, you have to hold this so that when I get up to the top the ladder doesn't wobble and cause me to fall."

I came down and asked her to stand in front of the ladder. "Now you curl your toes at the bottom." I showed her how.

"These are my new shoes!"

"What do you want?" I asked and laughed. "Do you want scratched shoes or a father with a broken leg?"

She wanted to run in and change shoes first, but it was almost time for guests. Impatiently I said, "No. Right now I don't care about your shoes. Just hold the ladder."

She held the ladder just as I had shown her. When

I reached the top, however, the old bulb broke as I was unscrewing it, and the metal section stayed in the outlet. I had to climb down the ladder, hurry inside the house, turn off the breaker, and grab pliers to unscrew the metal residue.

When I went back up, Rachel faithfully held the ladder. (She didn't scuff her shoes.) As I came down, I realized the importance of what she had done. To my daughter, holding the ladder had seemed like such a meaningless chore. To me, it was a safety issue. I would not have been able to change that light if she or someone had not held my ladder.

The higher we need to go, the more important ladder holders become.

As I put away my equipment, I thought, that's the way it works in the church and in the business world. The higher we need to go, the more important ladder holders become. It was one of those great moments of insight to me. I've always valued people, but in that instant, I realized the absolute necessity of seeking, recruiting, and training individuals to hold ladders or do any other leadership function.

Since that day in Queens, the message of holding ladders has become increasingly significant to me. As I travel around the country, I sometimes ask, "Who is holding your ladder?" I'm convinced that all successful painters who are able to reach high on the building do so because of those below who are steadying them while they work and fulfill their vision.

Those who insist on doing everything themselves can still paint—but not very high and not very

effectively. And because they insist on doing it themselves, it's not very safe or sensible.

What Kind Of Person Is Holding Your Ladder?

"I'm a nobody."

"I don't make any difference. No one even misses me when I'm absent."

"I just answer the telephone in our office and do a little word processing. Anybody can do what I do."

"I'm not a preacher or a singer, so I'm just one of the lesser lights in our church."

Those are typical of the kind of responses I've heard from individuals—the support people—those who are just as important in their own supporting roles as the stars of the show.

I want to be clear about identifying ladder holders.

- They are the foundation of any organization.
- They are the ones who allow leaders to reach their highest potential.
- They have the ladder held so securely that the leaders don't have to fret or constantly worry if they'll fall.

In the previous chapter I asked, "Who is holding your ladder?" Now I ask, what kind of person is holding your ladder? Let's look more closely at those we accept, enlist, recruit, or hire to hold our ladders.

The most obvious point is we can't just throw anybody into the job.

To give an idea of the importance of this role, I'll use myself as an example. I weigh about 155 pounds and I'm five feet eight, so I'm not a heavy person. Let's say you decide to climb a ladder that reaches twenty feet. I might be able to hold your ladder if the ground is totally level. What happens when you decide to ascend a forty-foot ladder? You don't want just anybody down at the bottom.

Ladder holders are the foundation of any organization. They are the ones who allow leaders to reach their highest potential.

At conferences, I often illustrate this. I look for one of the largest men in the audience and then ask him to come up to the platform and stand next to me.

I make certain he towers over me by at least six inches and weighs fifty or more pounds more than I do.

As the man stands next to me, the differences between us are too obvious to comment on. "If you were climbing a forty-foot ladder, whom would you choose to hold that ladder?" I ask the audience. Obviously, they always choose the other man.

"Look at me! I'm a great ladder holder," I say. "You don't know this, but I have a PhD in ladder holding. I love holding ladders. There's nothing I feel better about than doing just that. It gives me such deep joy and inner satisfaction. Besides that, I have learned beautiful techniques. Why, I can hold any ladder with two fingers and use only one foot. When I hold a ladder, I am so graceful, it looks as if I'm posing for a sculptor. Besides, I've held many ladders in my life. I have also held ladders in Kenya, India, and Australia, so I'm an international ladder holder. All right, a few ladders did shake a little, but so far no one has fallen—I mean, not yet."

I point to the man next to me. "You don't know anything about him and you haven't questioned him about his experience. Yet just looking at us, you'd rather have him hold your ladder when you have to climb forty feet high. Why would you choose this less-experienced person over me?"

"He's taller."

"He's stronger."

"He's bigger than you."

I don't blame the audience. If I had a choice, I'd want someone who is heavier and stronger than I am to be at the bottom of my ladder.

The principle works in any form of leadership. Leaders call for the bigger man because their lives are on the line. The higher the climb, the stronger the person they want at the bottom. That just makes common sense.

I also discovered that the audience didn't care about my education, and they didn't want to know that I could pose gracefully while I did my job. They wanted physical strength—assurance they would be safe when they reached thirty feet, forty, fifty, and even sixty.

> We need to pick the right people to do the job we want done.

"We want someone strong enough to hold the ladder so we can feel safe," someone usually yells out.

NEGATIVE QUALITIES

We don't always want to pick the person who is largest. It depends on the task. Strength is important, but often we have other qualities we need. One way to see this is to focus on the qualities we don't want.

What does this say to us who are in leadership roles?

We need to pick the right people to do the job we want done.

Here are the kinds of people we don't want to hold our ladders.

1. *We don't want those who need constant*

reminding. When I know I'm going to have to make a fifty-foot climb, what kind of person do I choose? As we think about the tasks in our church or business that need doing, whom will we ask?

It's stressful and frustrating if we have to say to someone on Sunday morning, "Don't forget. You promised to help me Tuesday night." What a chore it is if we have to call that same person two hours before the scheduled time and say, "I just wanted to remind you that we start at 7:30 tonight."

We have many people like that in our businesses and in our churches. For instance, I'll tell you about a man I'll call Hector. He had the nicest smile of anyone I've ever seen. "Would you come over Friday night and help?" I once asked. He agreed and promised that he wanted to do anything he could to help me.

It didn't take me long to realize that Hector would do anything—that is, if I reminded him enough times. This is slightly exaggerated, but it seemed that by Tuesday, I'd have to call and remind him what I wanted him to do. On Wednesday, I'd have to tell him what time I wanted him at the church. Thursday, I'd have to call again just to make sure he hadn't forgotten and planned to do something else.

> *I want to make sure that my ladder holder understands what I'm trying to accomplish.*

This doesn't apply only to Hector, because he has brothers and sisters—and the church and the marketplace is filled with them. If I make all the arrangements and then explain in simple detail, they'll do what I want. Some of them will come on the right day, but I can also expect them to arrive at least fifteen minutes late.

Others want to help, but I have to explain every step about how to do the job. It's the same job I explained three weeks earlier and will need to clarify again in another three weeks.

What do we say about people like Hector?

"By the time I get through telling him I might as well do it myself," is the common reaction.

Sometimes we're so tired of those who need constant reminding that we try to mount the steps by ourselves without any support. That's a mistake. We have focused so much on the negative ladder holders, we forget there are other, dependable individuals we can call on.

2. *We don't want those who behave casually.* Here's a question every business and church leader needs to ask: "Are the people I hire or recruit intentional about their work?" If Elmer holds my ladder will he curl all his toes and hold the ladder with both hands? Or will he have one hand draped casually across one of the rungs and a cup of Starbucks coffee in the other? Will he sip his coffee and carry on a conversation with someone across the street while I'm up there painting? I hope not. If Elmer is going to hold my ladder I want his total attention.

I want to make sure that my ladder holder understands what I'm trying to accomplish. Think of the various volunteer jobs in the church, such as being an usher. For example, I finished a conference in Albuquerque, New Mexico, on Saturday night and had planned to take the overnight flight back to Atlanta. Because of bad weather in the east, the flight was canceled and I could not get out until mid-day Sunday. I picked a church near the hotel and went inside.

Two ushers stood in the doorway chatting about a gospel concert one of them had attended. They both held bulletins in their hands. I paused, stared at them, but they were too involved to notice me. I waited a few seconds and asked, "May I have a bulletin?"

"Oh, sure," said one of them as he handed one to me and then took a step backward so that I could get through. As soon as I passed, the two men picked up their conversation. I wouldn't want either of them to be a ladder holder for me!

What about the people in the parking lot who direct traffic? As the lot gets full, are they alert to help people find space for their cars? What about the friendliness of our nursery workers? What about the minister of music or choir director? Do they care about serving or only performing?

How about the church office? Is the receptionist answering phones intentionally or casually? That is, does the receptionist make each caller feel special or act as if it's a minor intrusion on her time? Are people promptly returning their voice-mail messages?

Haven't most of us walked into an office and waited for several minutes while the receptionist finishes a personal call? I've even had receptionists ignore me when I say, "Excuse me." Sometimes without ever looking up at me the person behind the desk says sharply, "Just a minute." On one occasion a woman was filing her nails and barked at me, "Can't you see I'm busy?"

When I've spoken about such situations in conferences, one or two business people walk up to me later and refer to these negative qualities. They say something like, "That makes more sense for me than anything else." They realize the importance of the intentional focus of everyone in their organization.

3. *We don't want resumé builders.* Who are the resumé builders? They're the kinds who, while they're holding my ladder, aren't giving me their total attention. They're looking around at other things they'll do after they've finished with me. I'm only a temporary job until the real job comes along. They do the work—barely—but that's not their real area of interest. They're looking around for the brighter light, the shinier ladder, or the taller building. They're not committed to what they're doing now; they're thinking of what they want to do in their next position.

> *As leaders, we need to choose those who are committed to us.*

I want people to have their eyes on me while they hold my ladder. Too often, especially in the marketplace, those who are supposed to hold ladders are only holding on enough to appear to be working. They're working—but not on the ladder. They're positioning themselves for the next job.

This means that when we select ladder holders, as leaders, we need to choose those who are committed to us. If we're going to be forty feet in the air, we don't want someone who may wave as she leaves us and moves on to hold a larger ladder down the street while we're still up in the air.

4. *We don't want unhappy people.* I've never understood why somebody would keep going to the same church for thirty-eight years and leave mad every Sunday. Most of us know individuals like that in our church. We also know them in the market-place. They're unhappy when they come, and they're angry when they leave. The music will be too loud one week and not lively enough the next. The pastor prayed too long or didn't preach enough gospel.

Think of a situation like this. Suppose Amos goes to the ABC Barbeque on Friday night. He tells Pastor Green they have lousy food, slow service, and high prices."

"That's terrible," Pastor Green says.

The following week, Amos says, "I ate at the ABC Barbeque again Friday night. They still have lousy food, slow service, and high prices."

Every week Amos will complain about the restaurant but he won't stop going there. Doesn't someone need to say to him, "Go somewhere else to eat"? I've often said to pastors, "Some of your members could get their healing if they just parked their car at somebody else's church."

We don't apply the same common sense to the perpetual grumblers in our congregations. They've been unhappy for forty-three years. The chances aren't very good that they'll change.

5. *We don't want people just to agree.* When I was a pastor, I became aware of people who would agree with all my plans and ideas. "Oh, yes, yes, pastor," she might say. "I'll help you on the building plan. I'm there to help you with a new and more focused ministry to women, and I'll support you as you push that men's ministry." She also wants to help me with the youth choir.

Then, as the visionary leader, I started those projects. I started climbing the ladder, calmly and anxiety free. After all, she said she'd be there to support me. I'd get up fifteen feet and look down. She wasn't there! I'd start to move upward, trying to hold things steady, and realize that the higher I climbed the more help I needed at the bottom. I didn't know where she was, but if I could find her, I'm sure the conversation would start like this:

"You promised to hold my ladder."

"Yes, yes, of course, I'll help you. I know you're doing the right thing."

Five Core Qualities Of Ladder Holders

If I'm climbing, I want to be sure that my supporters know what I'm trying to do when I'm alone at the top with my paint buckets, brushes, and scrapers. Do those at the ground understand what I'm trying to accomplish? Do they realize that I can't paint over cracked paint because I must first chip away the old? Or do they get impatient and yell, "Just put a fresh coat over the old stuff"?

I also want to make this clear: Those who are

gripping the ladder don't have to agree with my tactics or methods. They do, however, need to understand where I want to go even if they would have taken a different route. They do have to believe in my vision and agree with where I'm going.

But what if they don't have the vision? What if they don't have any idea where I'm going? How much will I be able to depend on them and their commitment to my vision?

> *Those who are gripping the ladder don't have to agree with my tactics or methods. They do have to believe in my vision and agree with where I'm going.*

For example, let's say I visit Joyful Tidings Church next Sunday morning and they have 100 people in the worship service. I wait outside until church service is over. I hold a tape recorder in my hand. As each person steps forward I ask, "What's the vision of this church?"

How many answers will I get? Could I count on twenty people out of the hundred to give me the same answer? I don't mean a memorized statement or something simplistic such as "Our vision is to save souls." The church may not have an evangelistic program and no one has joined the church in two years, but is that still the vision? Not likely.

What happens at Joyful Tidings Church when I ask? If they don't know the vision, how can they be in tune with the pastor? They may love the pastor and nod appreciatively at the sermons every week. They may enjoy the music program and feel inspired by the worship. But that's still moving in the realm of projects. The sermon is a project; the music is a project. *What is the vision?*

Because I raised that issue myself several times, I started asking myself a question. *If I had to find a ladder holder what core qualities would I seek?* What would they have to have for me to consider them as class A, number one, top-notch, eagle, ladder holders?

I came up with five qualities I'd insist on. There are others I'd like to see and that I would hope for. But these are the essentials for ladder holders.

The first quality is *strength*. They have to be strong. By that, I mean they must be people who can handle instruction and criticism, with whom I can use plain language and not have to walk on eggshells and fix things for them. That means that if they need to be corrected in certain areas they can change them without my having to worry about how much I'm going to hurt their feelings.

I'm not referring to being crass, rude, arrogant, or obnoxious. For example, let's focus on the person running the sound system. Last Sunday morning the sound system reverberated at times and caused me to shudder. At other times, the amplification was so low that people strained to hear what I said.

I don't want excuses or lengthy explanation, and this is more important than whether the sound engineer slept well the night before. This is ministry—service—to the body of Jesus Christ.

"The sound wasn't right," I need to be able to say

and then add, "Do whatever you have to do to make it happen. People can't worship when they have to clamp their hands over their ears."

I expect the sound engineer to know how to take care of those things. When I speak that way, I'm not trying to hurt feelings; I'm just conducting business.

In the church, however, we know that some members are so fragile we can hardly correct them without their getting upset. "I'm doing my best, you know," they may say. "Why are you always picking on me? Why don't you like me? Why do you find fault with everything I do?"

We need strong ladder holders—those strong enough to take criticism and who want to do better.

> **We need strong ladder holders; those strong enough to take criticism and who want to do better.**

To use the ladder image again, I can't be sixty feet in the air and have to yell down to remedy the mistakes my holder is making. I need someone strong enough to do the task right and to be secure enough that I can yell down instructions and know the person will listen.

Another way I explain this is to say, "The greater the need, the shorter the prayer." If I were drowning I wouldn't say, "Oh God, The Everlasting Father of Abraham, Isaac, and Jacob, the Almighty One who was, is, and ever shall be, hallowed be thy name, seeth thou that I drownest? Throwest me a rope that I may cling to safely even as I am always safe in the old rugged cross."

No, I'm going to scream, "Help, God!" I won't worry about whether I addressed the entire Trinity or only Jesus. I won't be concerned about whether I concluded with "In Jesus' Name Amen." I'm too busy trying to stay alive!

Hence, the greater the need, the shorter the prayer. And when I'm up there on a forty-foot ladder the need is great. It's not an option—I must have people holding the ladder who can handle instructions in two to three words and be able to do it quickly.

The second quality is *attentiveness*. They need to be able to pay attention, be alert to what I'm saying and absorb it quickly. I don't want to give them the same lessons repeatedly.

Can't we assume that if James and Martha have been ushering for twenty-seven years, they ought to know what they're supposed to do? Those who clean the church ought to know where every wastebasket is. Those who sing in the choir ought to know the time they're supposed to be there to rehearse on Wednesday night and what time they're expected to be in their robes on Sunday morning.

We don't have to chase after attentive people repeatedly. They understand the first time.

The third quality is *faithfulness*. I'm not referring to having faith in the Lord. That's assumed if they're going to serve in the church. I'm talking about having faith in me as their leader and being committed to me.

I learned very early in my own ministry that if they aren't faithful to me—if they aren't committed to the same vision I am—they'll abandon me. The worst thing is that they run away, not before I start and not when I explain what I want. They nod, smile, and agree, but as soon as I'm fifteen feet away, they abandon me.

I need people who remain at the ladder no matter how difficult things become. As long as I'm up there, the faithful show me that I can be assured they're down below. They don't need my constantly yelling down, "You're doing a great job. You're wonderful." They're steady and I know I can count on them.

The fourth quality is *firmness*. By that I mean not exploited by manipulative people. In every church and in every corporation there are manipulative types. Al Qaeda terrorists aren't new—only the name. Terrorism in the church is nothing new, but it's usually cloaked in ecclesiastical language, hidden in the by-laws, or made to sound spiritual and appealing. The ultimate goal of church terrorists is control and destruction. That sounds harsh, I'm sure, but that's what they're after.

They may speak in pious language such as, "The Holy Spirit led me," or say, "The Lord spoke to my heart." They may be extremely self-deceived or just mean spirited. It doesn't matter which because the end is the same. They want to destroy the present plans and operations. They do it in so many ways, but the one I've noticed most often is what I call *seductive manipulation*.

An illustration may help—and it's an embarrassing one at that. My first serious awareness of seductive manipulation came about when I was a twenty-six-year-old assistant pastor of a church in Oregon. A few of the leaders began to call me aside. They flattered me and told me how much they admired my ministry and loved my commitment.

"You know, we really enjoy it when you preach. When you're in the pulpit we get something out of the service," they would say and throw their arms around me. "We wish you could preach every Sunday and every Tuesday."

Until then I had never thought of such a thing. I had come to assist the senior pastor.

"You feed us when you preach or teach. You're anointed and you understand. The pastor just doesn't speak to us. His messages are all right, but they're just not relevant to our needs."

This kind of conversation didn't happen just once, but over a period of weeks. I was young, naïve, and egocentric. Very stupidly, I allowed them to manipulate me by their constant ego stroking. Instead of being the faithful ladder holder I should have been I started enjoying those conversations. At first, I listened and thanked them. When I walked away, I'd feel really special and anointed.

It wasn't long before I participated in the conversations. "You're right. He just doesn't understand the needs of people today."

I still remember at a business meeting where there was a particularly important item on the agenda. Several of the elders—the ones who had been stroking my ego—had convinced me that the plan the pastor wanted to put into action was unwise. He spoke and explained exactly what he wanted to see happen.

"May I say something?" I asked. When the pastor nodded, I stood up. I strongly disagreed with everything he had said. Point by point, I argued against what he wanted done. My seductive manipulators had done a good job on me.

I was wrong. I think I knew that thirty seconds after I began to speak. However, I didn't know how to back down and say, "I'm sorry." My words carried, and we vetoed something the pastor was committed to. I should have been his senior ladder holder and I had not only waffled, but I had worked against him. I wasn't the firm assistant he deserved.

God has a way of evening things out. The following year when I was a pastor in Michigan, I reaped the fruit of the bad seed I had sown in Oregon. I was then the senior pastor and the same type of seductive manipulators moved in on my territory.

Through that sad experience, I learned three important lessons:

1. If we disagree with our leader we don't do so publicly. We need to discuss it with that person in private.

2. If we disagree, we ought to search our motives before we speak. We need to be sure that others don't set us up. They won't speak up themselves, but they will find naïve and trusting souls to do the work for them.

3. If we disagree, we should be sure we don't do it

for personal gain. I didn't get it at the time, but those manipulators had instilled a desire in me to become the senior pastor. Because of them, I coveted a position that God had not called me to.

As I've thought with much shame about my behavior in Oregon, I realized— too late—that my agenda was not that I disagreed and wanted to express my viewpoint. My secret agenda was that I wanted to look smarter, brighter, and better informed than the senior pastor. Those seductive manipulators were using me—just as Satan used Eve in the Garden of Eden. And just like Eve, I was too naïve to realize what was going on—until it was too late.

> **1. If we disagree with our leader we don't do so publicly.**
> **2. If we disagree, we ought to search our motives before we speak**
> **3. If we disagree, we should be sure we don't do it for personal gain.**

The final quality is _loyalty_. I do not mean they must agree all the time. Loyalty doesn't mean repeating, "Yes, yes, yes," no matter what the visionary says.

I have formulated three sentences that explain what I mean.

1. You may disagree with my head but not my heart.

2. You may disagree with how I do things but not why I do things.

3. You may disagree with my methods but not my motivations.

CHAPTER THREE

PASTOR OR CEO

> The five essential qualities we seek:
> 1. **Strength.** They have to be people who can handle instruction and criticism.
> 2. **Attentiveness.** They ought to be alert to what I'm saying and absorb it quickly. I don't want to give them the same lessons repeatedly.
> 3. **Faithfulness.** They must have faith in me as their leader and be committed to me. If they aren't faithful to me—if they aren't committed to the same vision I am—they'll abandon me
> 4. **Firmness.** Manipulative people won't be able to exploit them.
> 5. **Loyalty.** They don't always have to agree, but (1) They may disagree with my head but not my heart. (2) They may disagree with how I do things but not why I do things. (3) They may disagree with my methods but not my motivations.

When I first went to Beulah Heights Bible College as president in 1989, I didn't have a background in human resources. We had seven people on our staff at that time—four of them part time and three full time. (Fourteen years later, we had more than ninety people on staff.) Over the years I've learned a few lessons about ladder holders that might be helpful to those who hire and fire.

Although my experience has been largely with personnel at Beulah Heights Bible College, these principles carry through in pastoral situations as well. Almost any week in the year, I have conversations with pastors who have problems with paid staff. They have a difficult job today. On one hand, they are pastors—that means they're shepherds who care for the sheep. On the other hand, they are the Chief Executive Officers (CEOs) and the congregation holds them responsible for the smooth running business of the church.

The first thing I've learned is that even though they are both pastor and CEO, they can't be both at the same time. I try to help them understand the difference between the two and when to give priority to one and when to the other.

It may help if I explain it this way. Let's say I'm the senior minister at First Spiritual Church. To every paid staff member, I am the CEO first and the pastor second. That means I must first do the business of the church with them. When I have accomplished that,

> *Even though they are both pastor and CEO, they can't be both at the same time.*

I can function as their pastor. If I get the order wrong, I am in trouble and so is the organization.

To every church member, I am the pastor first and the CEO second. I must be able to reach out to them as those who need to be nurtured, strengthened, encouraged, rebuked, and disciplined. When I've performed my pastoral duties, I can function as the CEO. If I get this wrong, then it's back to the matter of putting projects before people. If I see the members only as the means to accomplish what I want done, then I'll manipulate, threaten, coerce, or flatter them into fulfilling my agenda.

When I function as CEO with paid employees, the first lesson we learned is that we hire people for *what* they know; we fire them for *who* they are.

We may hire the musician because she can make the simplest music sound like a concerto in every piece she plays. We fire her because she has a bad attitude. We hire an office manager because he is a computer whiz and understands spreadsheets, profit and loss, government regulations, and knows all the latest software. We fire him because he can't get along with people.

What do we do when it's time to put someone on staff? My suggestion is that we need to re-think our policy. We want competent people, obviously. But when we select ladder holders, we need to spend more time with *who* they are rather than *what* they know.

I can read their resumés and I can talk to people they've worked for and with. That is important. But I also know that troubles in the job usually start over personality issues and not over competency. Once hired, they will give me joy or grief. With few exceptions, the people I have fired I have terminated because of their attitudes. Rarely have I had to get rid of someone for lack of ability to do the job.

> *We hire people for what they know; we fire them for who they are.*

This leads me to the second lesson I've learned: *Hire slowly and fire quickly.*

It's better to have a vacancy than to have bad help. Suppose the doctor diagnoses you with cancer, says surgery is the only option, and asks, "When would you want it scheduled?"

I'm guessing you'll say, "As soon as possible."

As a leader, a good question to ask ourselves is this, Why do I tolerate incompetent staff? Why do I allow them to infect the rest of the staff with their bad attitude? Here is the way I like to say it: Don't rush hiring decisions; don't delay firing decisions.

The third lesson I've learned is this: *The best time to fire somebody is the first time it goes through your head.* We tend to get our roles confused again here. Instead of thinking as a CEO and for the good of the organization, we tend to switch to our pastoral role and figure out ways to excuse or overlook problems serious enough that we'd consider terminating them.

Hire slowly and fire quickly. Don't rush hiring decisions; don't delay firing decisions.

I've also learned that if the situation is serious enough to fire people and we don't, after that we begin to search for reasons to keep them.

About the time I figured out this third lesson, I spotted an advertisement in *USA Today* [1] by Randall Murphy, the founder and president of the Acclivus Corporation. I don't know much about Acclivus except that their clients include major organizations such as Dunn and Bradstreet, Exxon, Mobile, Dell, FedEx, Dr. Pepper/Seven-Up and Roadway Express. The ad read: "When you are assigned the task of taking the hill—or the market—you are less concerned about who is *for* you and more concerned about who is *with* you."

Those words impacted me and I read the sentence several times. I've translated Murphy's statement into the business of the church such as when a congregation starts a new building program.

Those who make pledges are *for* us; those who
✝ pay their pledges are *with* us. We don't have to be
involved with churches very long before we recognize
that there is a large gap between those two groups.

Just because people say, "I'm for you," that isn't
the real issue. The real issue is what happens in
their lives. Do they do what they promise? Do they
faithfully follow their words by their actions?

THREE LEVELS OF LADDER HOLDERS

I've already mentioned the five things we have to
watch for that tell us who those ladder holders are.
From there, I started thinking about what happens with ladder holders in a church.

> *The best time to fire somebody is the first time it goes through your head... If the situation is serious enough to fire people and we don't, we begin to search for reasons to keep them.*

I concluded that there are three levels of ladder holders.

First, there are the *followers.* This word can refer to everybody in the congregation.

Second are the *ministers.* They feel God has called them, empowered them, and gifted them to serve in the church. When I use the word minister, I don't mean ordained ministers and pastors, although it may include them—I refer to all of those who have a heart to serve others.

Third are *leaders.* They minister through others. They don't have only a sense of calling; they also

have passion—and that passion is to see God work ✝
through others. True leaders don't try to deceive
themselves into thinking they can or even want to do
everything. They're willing to empower and trust
others. Ministers do service primarily by themselves;
leaders do service through others.

Throughout my years of serving in the church, we
have ruined many good ministers by shoving them
into leadership. Here's an example of what I mean. Let's say that
Josh has a passion for doing
prison ministry. He's also gifted
because he knows how to connect
with the incarcerated. They listen to him because they trust
him. On his own and without
anyone from the church behind
him, Josh goes to the local jail
every Friday and Saturday. He
does this out of concern and love.
He carries Gospel portions with

*Those who make
pledges are for us;
those who pay their
pledges are with us.
We don't have to
be involved with
churches very long
before we recognize
that there is a large
gap between those
two groups.*

him and teaches prisoners how to read the New
Testament. He sings, he preaches, and he takes time
to counsel with anyone who asks him to.

After two years, Josh has an amazing array of
results, such as several people believing in Jesus
Christ. Some of them have joined the church.
Everyone recognizes the value of Josh's ministry.

One day the pastor says, "We need to start an
official prison ministry through our church. Josh is
already doing it, so let's put him in charge."

"Every time we take prayer requests," an elder says, "Josh asks us to pray for the prison ministry and the prisoners."

"He regularly sends e-mails about the people who got saved," says a deacon.

"He's passionate about it," says one.

The board agrees unanimously.

That decision may sound like a good idea, but in the ten minutes they took to make that official verdict, they ruined Josh and his ministry.

There are three levels of ladder holders
1. Followers. This word can refer to everybody in the congregation.
2. Ministers. They feel God has called them, empowered them, and gifted them to serve.
3. Leaders. They minister through others.

Until then, Josh had been an excellent minister for God. He did an outstanding job as long as he was the only one who did the work. He has a tender heart and people instinctively trust him.

Yet his ministry has been ruined, because Josh has moved from ministry to leadership. He's no longer person-centered. He's overwhelmed with recruiting musicians and evangelists. He's constantly scheduling who will go to which jail and at what time. He must spend an immense amount of time teaching those who have volunteered for ministry. They need to understand appropriate behavior and what they can and can't do for the prisoners. He has to explain, for instance, that they can't carry mail in or out for those incarcerated. They can't give advice, especially not legal advice. Several times he has had to go to the sheriff and apologize for mistakes his people make.

After four months, Josh realizes that he has to manage and lead people. He no longer has a ministry. His passion starts to dry up. The well-meaning church board has ruined him. He's pouring his efforts into holding the ladder for others and he needs to be climbing his own ladder.

> *Ministers do service primarily by themselves; leaders do service through others.*

This comes down to saying that even though someone like Josh is doing an exemplary ministry, it doesn't mean he can function well as a good ladder holder.

TRAINING LADDER HOLDERS

This leads me to emphasize that ladder holders need to be *trained.* Very few ministers have qualified and trained ladder holders. I've held conversations with pastors of large churches all over this country. I point out the qualities I've already mentioned. They need people who are strong, attentive, faithful, firm, and loyal.

Then I say, "Name your ladder holders. I'm not asking for positions and titles such as deacons or trustees. Think about those five qualities I gave you." I pause and then say, "Tell me the names of your ladder holders."

No matter how many times I've done this, the highest anybody has been able to name is five. The size of the congregation doesn't seem to matter, whether it's a church of 100 members or one with more than 10,000.

When the pastors can't get beyond a few names, it tells me that the church has done an excellent job of raising followers but has been abysmal about doing leadership development.

At the beginning of this book, I mentioned that developing people takes time, and time is one thing we don't have in our busy lives.

Ladder holders need to be trained.

I also remind pastors that their armor bearers or assistants may not necessarily be ladder holders. Just because somebody is an assistant pastor, assistant choir director, vice president of the corporation, or has an impressive title doesn't make him or her a trusted ladder holder.

To make this clear, I try to get pastors to think of situations when the church is filled with problems and ask, "To whom would you turn for help?"

They still stare at me in confusion, so here's an illustration that has seemed to make clear what I mean.

"Let's say you are marooned on an island. The battery on your cell phone is running low. You decide you have just enough juice to make one call. Let's also say that you know that no member of your family is available." Then I pause and ask, "Whom will you call?"

They easily eliminate the ones they wouldn't call, and some of them are prominent in the church. They finally realize that they need to call a true ladder holder—a person who is faithful and someone who is committed to them personally. Those are the individuals who will do whatever necessary to get them off the island.

"When you are assigned the task of taking the hill—or the market—you are less concerned about who is for you and more concerned about who is with you."

If you were marooned on that island, who is the ladder holder you'd call?

How Do We Recruit Volunteers?

"Who will hold my ladder?" That's a common way for us to get help. We look around, cry out to whomever will come to our aid, and welcome them, regardless of their abilities. We may not put it that way. Instead we announce, "We need two new Sunday school teachers. Who will serve for one year?" Or we plead for men to join the choir.

That method works! People volunteer and we get results. There's just one serious problem—it's the wrong approach.

My advice is simple. *Stop asking for volunteers.*

I'll explain the reason.

When I was a pastor and asked for volunteers, the people who couldn't do the job always raised their hands. I appreciated their zeal, but they simply couldn't do what I needed done.

People who couldn't sing rushed to join the choir. People who had forgotten how to smile volunteered to usher. People who disliked children raised their hands to keep the nursery. People who couldn't teach committed themselves to take a Sunday school class.

I also realized another problem. Within a short time, those who volunteer so readily are just as ready to un-volunteer. They seem to hear the Holy Spirit whisper "I send you" every time the pastor calls for help. After a few weeks, they also seem to hear the same Holy Spirit whisper, "Your work here is finished." Not that they accomplished anything productive, but at least they leave. In reality, they shouldn't have volunteered in the first place.

> *That is the question; that is also the problem. How do we un-volunteer a volunteer?*

The bigger problem occurs when those inept-but-well-meaning helpers get into their position and then we have to ask, "How do you get rid of them?"

That is the question; that is also the problem. How do we un-volunteer a volunteer? There isn't much chance that the bass in the choir who can't hit a C below middle C will ever learn. The grumbling nursery staff person won't suddenly love to change diapers.

Suppose we read the headline in tomorrow's newspaper that says the local public schools seek volunteers to teach English, science, and math. Would I want my children to attend a school where all

We need to view volunteers as unpaid staff.

instructors are volunteers? The public wouldn't stand for it. "We want professionals teaching our children," they would insist.

Why is it that we staff our Christian Education departments, our ushering committees, and our nurseries with volunteers? Could it be that reading, writing, and arithmetic are a lot more important than real issues of life such as preparing for heaven or personal integrity? We keep doing what the church has been doing for the past hundred years: we print notices in the bulletin, the newsletter, the church's website: we need four teachers for the children's department.

Surely there must be a better way.

And there is!

We need to view volunteers as unpaid staff.

I've come to the conclusion that the most-qualified people are waiting to be recruited. They don't rush to sign up on the legal pad hanging on a bulletin board. They don't call the worship leader's cell phone. They're there, available, and they're willing to serve *if they're asked*. We need to learn how to recruit volunteers.

CHAPTER FOUR

THE BIBLE AND VOLUNTEERS

Have you ever wondered what the Bible says about volunteerism?

From the time of the Old Testament all the way up to John the Baptist, followers generally chose their leader. People would hear a great prophet, listen to him, do whatever he told them, and become his disciple.

Something changed, however, after John the Baptist. The next leader on the world scene was Jesus. Followers didn't choose Jesus; Jesus chose followers. I wonder how many people think about that. Each of the Gospel accounts tells us how Jesus went about his ministry. One of His first acts was to choose those He wanted to follow Him and they were the ones He trained. (See Mark 1:16-20 and Luke 5:1-11.)

> **Followers didn't choose Jesus; Jesus chose followers.**

Sometimes people offered to follow Jesus and He turned them down. Here are two examples. "A certain man said unto him, 'Lord, I will follow thee whithersoever thou goest,' and Jesus said unto him, 'Foxes have holes, and birds of the air have nests; but the Son of Man hath not where to lay his head'" (Luke 12:57-58). Jesus said no.

Another time, Jesus set a man free from demons and afterward the healed man wanted to go with the Lord. Jesus said no. (See Mark 5:18-19.)

Jesus held a powerful vision of his ladder that

stretched from earth to heaven. He didn't want just anyone supporting him. In fact, just before his betrayal, Jesus said to his disciples: "You have not chosen me, but I have chosen you, and ordained you, that ye should go and bring forth fruit, and that your fruit should remain" (John 15:16a).

At no place in Jesus' ministry do we read that he stood up and said, "I need helpers to do the work. I want fifty people to follow me." Instead, Jesus recruited volunteers who would hold that ladder firm no matter how hard the forces of evil struck.

Instead of seeking people to volunteer, wise leaders follow the Lord's example and seek out the gifted. As a pastor and as president of a growing Bible college, I know that I must have gifted people in all the key positions if we're going to be successful. Yes, I've made mistakes, but I've made many good decisions too. I watch for those who show that "extra something"—call it a gift or a unique quality—but there are individuals who have that special spark that sets them apart. Those are the ones I want to develop.

In the New Testament, Paul writes several times about spiritual gifts. Although he lists nine of them in 1 Corinthians 11, he doesn't give the entire catalogue of abilities. Obviously, there are gifts he didn't mention, but the point is the same. If we want something to happen, we rely on those who are talented, gifted, and who can make it happen. We don't sit around and hope they'll knock on our doors. Like Jesus did, we go after them and say, "We want you. We have a place for you."

It's also interesting that those Jesus recruited had to decide if they wanted to follow him, even after they were asked. In Luke 9:59-62, Jesus asked a man to follow Him. The man protested that he had to go home and bury his father. Jesus said, "Let the dead bury their dead: but go thou and preach the kingdom of God" (v.60).

"And another also said, 'Lord, I will follow thee; but let me first go bid them farewell, which are at home at my house.' And Jesus said unto him, 'No man, having put his hand to the plough, and looking back, is fit for the kingdom of God'" (verses 61-62).

It's also interesting that Paul exhorts the Thessalonians, "And we beseech you, brethren, to know them which labour among you, and are over you in the Lord, and admonish you" (1 Thessalonians 5:12). The only time I hear anyone quote that verse is during ordination services. That fits, of course, but it has a much wider application.

In the first chapter of this book, I pointed out three ways to do the work of the church and the third is to develop others—to teach them to do what they can do. I also pointed out that it takes time for that to happen. It means working with those ladder holders and instructing them how to do an excellent job. Some may be best at holding short ladders and others taller ones. Some may work best alone and others in groups. The principle still remains the same: leaders need to develop others.

I know that in larger congregations it becomes difficult for the pastors to know everyone. By the time a church has ten thousand members, the senior pastor probably doesn't know more than 10 percent of them. It simply means they have many ladders and many painters, and they need an even larger support force behind those painters.

True leaders develop their own followers—I'll say more about that in the next chapter. Wise leaders assimilate people by recognizing their gifts and placing them in the right role. They have files on who can do what function. When we need chaperones to go with our youth group on a field trip, if we're smart, we don't send out a call and ask, "Who's going to help?" Just because they are parents doesn't mean they would make appropriate chaperones.

> **Wise leaders assimilate people by recognizing their gifts and placing them in the right role.**

There may be those who don't have time or inclination to work with the youth department every week. But if we know their capabilities and call on them two or three times a year when we have special events going on, they're likely to say, "Yes, I can help."

It's not a hopeless task to find out who is talented. With great computer programs available, when we do intake we can do a gifts inventory, we can do the passion inventory, or a calling inventory.

When a new member says, "I love organizing short-term projects," that's important for us to put on file. When we get ready to put out a new church directory, for example, that's a short-term project.

That person can organize and make the operation run smoothly. That is the same person who won't be available for tasks that go on every week throughout the year.

Here's an example. I spoke at a leadership conference in Boston at the New Covenant Christian Church where Bishop Gilbert Thompson, a visionary, is the senior pastor. Bishop Thompson sat in the front row with an open laptop typing notes as fast as he could. He didn't want to miss any significant information. I remember seeing the smile on his face when I talked about not asking for volunteers.

> **We need different ladder holders for different levels of ministry.**

Months later Bishop Thompson's assistant said that one significant factor "has revolutionized our ministry. We don't ask for volunteers any more—we recruit them."

Is it any wonder that New Covenant Christian Church has dozens of high level ladders up?

IMPORTANT ISSUES, IMPORTANT RECRUITING

Think about volunteers this way. You are a leader. You're only four feet off the ground, but you're climbing the rungs. As you gaze upward, you know you're capable of reaching a height of at least sixty feet.

As you start to ascend, are you going to cry out,

"People of God, someone—anyone—come and hold this ladder?" Not likely. If you're a wise leader, you will already have chosen (or recruited) someone you trust. You want to reach as high as your ladder will go and not worry whether the person at the bottom is going to lose interest or walk away.

When we're training ladder holders, those learners need clear instruction. Church folk don't take hints and the best way to understand this is to think about church announcements.

As leaders, we can put all the information in the bulletin and the newsletter. We can tell them individually in person, make phone calls, send out e-mails, proclaim it from the pulpit, and write an announcement for the overhead or power point. It doesn't matter what we do or how often we send out the information, people will still phone the church office. "What time was that meeting? Was it nine or nine-thirty? Was it Monday or Tuesday?"

When we're developing ladder holders, however, we train them the right way. A good way to look at this is from the book of Proverbs. Although much of the instruction reads as if it's a father giving advice to a son, scholars have seen this differently. The advice and instruction is intended for scholars in training. The instructors looked upon them as students or sons. These are instructions in personal growth and leadership.

In the oft-quoted Proverbs 22:6, it reads: "Train up a child in the way he should go: and when he is old, he will not depart from it." If we apply this (and

I think this is the right way) to students or scholars receiving instructions, it means that if we who are leaders train new people properly—that is, when we do it right and do it in the beginning—we'll produce the right kind of results. It also means we won't have to take a lot of correctional action later. If a tree starts growing right the first time, we don't have to spend all kinds of time trying to straighten it out. When we're talking about ladder holders, we know they must be properly trained and developed.

BEFORE CLIMBING LADDERS

Joseph Campbell once said that one of the great tragedies in life is to climb to the top of the ladder only to find that our ladder is leaning against the wrong wall. He meant that too many people take what he called the prudent path in life and yet they miss the joy. He said they never discover their bliss.

How do we avoid that problem? How do we help ourselves and others discover our bliss?

Before we start climbing we have to do three things:

1. *We need to decide where we want to go.* We need to be sure of our reason for being on the ladder in the first place. What tools do we need to do the job for which we're climbing the ladder? What tools will we need when we get up there? One thing I learned during my student days when I painted was that it was just too tiring and time consuming to go up and down that ladder. I had to make sure I had

everything ready before I started up.

2. *We need to be clear about our vision.* We need to be able to tell our ladder holders why we're up there and why they're working hard. If we get really high and the ladder sways, we had better be sure we know why we're there. When we go through those turbulent times—and we all do—we'd better be clear about our reason for being so high off the ground. We also need to make it clear to those who support us so that they'll know why they're doing their jobs.

> **Leaders ask what and why; followers ask how and when.**

Leaders ask two questions. I mentioned this in my book *Futuring* [2], but I think it's important to say it again here.

Leaders ask *what* and *why*; followers ask *how* and *when*. Every effective leader needs to understand this.

Leaders must first define the what—that which they want done. Once they know that answer they need to be clear on why: Why are we doing this?

In my book, *Futuring* [3], I gave this illustration. At Beulah Heights Bible College we wanted to reach out and start a curriculum for students for whom English was not their first language. That was a *what*—the curriculum.

Why do we want to do that? We answer, because the mission of the institution, even in its earliest days was to reach unreached groups. *Why*? There are increasingly large numbers of people for whom

English is a second language and we need to reach them. *Why?* Because they represent another market. *Why?* Because the place of missions has changed. There are more other-country born missionaries in America today than there are missionaries from America in other countries. *Why?* Because they don't have to get visas and they have natural built bridges, their credibility is in place, and their language is in place.

> **Before we start climbing we have to do three things:**
> **1. We need to decide where we want to go**
> **2. We need to be clear about our vision.**
> **3. We need to ask ourselves: What are we doing to prepare ourselves as better communicators?**

3. We need to ask ourselves: what are we doing to prepare ourselves as better communicators?

During the summer breaks when I was a student at Beulah Heights Bible College, I earned my living as a painter. I've always said that I did it to pay my bills not because it was my idea of a higher calling.

I remember many times I'd get tired of moving up and down. The first few days I'd forgotten a tool or realized I needed something else and would have to go back down to get it. That was not only tiring, but it was inefficient.

Because I learned that lesson quite well, I teach it this way at conferences. I'll often ask if there are any in the audience who have done professional painting. Two or three people usually raise their hands, so I ask them to join me.

"Pretend I'm going to paint the second story of a house," I say to them. "It's way up there, the paint is peeling, and it's in pretty bad shape. I'm getting ready to go up on a forty-foot ladder. I don't want to go up and down repeatedly, so tell me what I need in my tool belt before I go up."

"You'll need a scraper and wire brush," one will say.

"You'll need sandpaper and a hammer."

One of them will mention a nail setter because there are always nails poking out. Someone will mention a caulking gun.

"You'll need paint and a brush and at least one rag to wipe away any smears you make," one of them will say.

I smile because they have it exactly right. "Now, if you're climbing a forty-foot ladder as a Sunday school teacher. You want to be an excellent Sunday school teacher. What tools do you need to put in your tool belt?"

Then I ask, "Is there anybody here who's a Sunday school teacher? Come on up." After they come up—and there are always a lot of them—I ask, "Are you a good Sunday school teacher?"

Besides smiles and a few giggles, they answer, "Yes."

"Can you become a better Sunday school teacher?"

The answer is always, "Yes!"

"For you to be a better Sunday school teacher

what all do you have to do?" Then I wait for them to respond.

They always start off with "I need to pray more and I need to read the Bible more."

Everyone nods and I say, "Yes, that's good, but what else do you need to do?" Before the teachers respond, people from the audience yell out, "Read more books."

I ask them to name a few books and they do. Then they start adding things such as, a concordance, a Bible dictionary, a Bible encyclopedia, and different versions of the Bible.

We could ask the same questions for any position in the church. What I want them to think about is this: What must I do if I'm going to be a better, more effective communicator?

I also remind church leaders that whenever we get up to preach, we need to remind ourselves that we have five generations facing us.

How effective am I at reaching them? For us to be more effective, what are we putting in our tool kits on communication skills, story telling skills, movement, hand gestures, body language, and vocabulary? What are we reading that puts us in touch with the now generation?

It's also important to remind ourselves that everyone is not a leader. God doesn't call all of us that way. Even though we know that, some of us in leadership positions may be trying to fulfill jobs that we're not suited for.

Maybe we need to become managers.

LEADERSHIP ISSUE	SENIORS	BUILDERS	BOOMERS	BUSTERS (GEN-X)	MOSAICS (NEXTERS)
Era Born	Before 1928	1929 - 1945	1946 - 1964	1965 - 1983	1984 - X
Life Paradigm	Manifest Destiny	Be grateful you have a job	You owe me	Relate to me	Life is cafeteria
Attitude toward Authority	Respect	Endure	Replace	Ignore	Choose
Role of Relationships	Long Term	Significant, useful	Limited, caring	Central	Global
Value System	Traditional	Conservative	Self-based	Changing	Shop around
Role of Career	Loyal, responsible	Means for living	Central focus	Irritant	Always changing
Schedules	What's up?	Mellow	Frantic	Aimless	Volatile
Technology	What's that?	Hope to outlive it	Master it	Enjoy it	Employ it
View of the Future	Uncertain	Seek to stabilize	Create it!	Hopeless	??

5

Are We Managing Ladders?

Are you a leader? Or has God gifted you to be a manager? This is important to figure out which we are and where we belong.

Leaders know where they want to reach. They point up toward the spot that's so high those standing next to them don't always see it.

Managers know exactly where to position the ladder for the maximum benefit. They may not see that special spot the leaders gaze at, but they can figure out how to make everything work so leaders can ascend the steps and not have to look back and worry if they have solid support.

First, I want to make it clear that leaders aren't superior and neither are managers. One is not more important than the other; however, they are different. The grid below distinguishes between leaders and managers. We need managers just as surely as

LEADERS	MANAGERS
Emphasize what and why	Emphasize how and when
Work from the future back to the present	Work from the past to the present
Focus on the long term	Focus on the short term or immediate
Embrace a macro-perspective	Embrace a micro-perspective
Favor innovative thinking	Favor routine/safe thinking
Seek to balance idealism with realism	Emphasize pragmatism over idealism
Show revolutionary flair	Protect status quo
Clarify the vision Inspire and motivate	Implement the vision
Excite others by change	Are threatened by change
Decide quickly	Decide slowly
Identify opportunities	Identify obstacles
Take risks	Avoid risks
Pursue resources	Actions limited to available resources
People centered	System centered
Idea centered	Plan centered
Centered on core issues	Distracted by peripheral issues
Want others' approval	Need others' approval
Do the right thing	Do things right

we need leaders.

No matter how great and visionary leaders are, unless they have managers on their team, they won't get very far.

Second, we need to recognize which one we are, because if we're leaders in managers' positions we're frustrated and ineffective. We'll constantly see better ways to do things or lose patience with those who methodically work out details. Just as true, if we're managers in leaders' positions we're killing our organization. We're busy seeing that things function properly and that all lights are put out at night and that we don't overpay our creditors. If that's where we are, we don't have time, energy, or ability to dream about the future.

If we're managers, we pride ourselves on being practical.

OBSERVATIONS ABOUT LEADERS AND MANAGERS

- Leaders and managers complement each other.
- Both need to work in the area of their strengths.
- Successful managers aren't always successful leaders; successful leaders aren't necessarily successful managers.
- We need to evaluate the success of managers differently from the success of leaders.
- We consider managers successful when they operate the organization efficiently as well as deliver services on time and within budget.
- We consider leaders successful when they enable their organization to grow in its ability to serve the community by discovering new needs, expanding the resources base, and innovating approaches to service delivery, and when they energize or transform the organization.

By contrast, if we're leaders, we pride ourselves on being imaginative and visionary.

Third, if we're supervisors in charge of people, we want to figure out the kind of ladder holders we need. Sometimes a situation calls for another leader and sometimes a manager. If we're leaders, we'll learn to recognize individual gifts.

Instead of going into detail on this, if you want to know more about this, please see my book *Futuring: Leading Your Church into Tomorrow* (Baker Books, 2002, pages 123-128).

> **Leaders know where they want to reach. Managers know exactly where to position the ladder for the maximum benefit.**

Here's an interesting difference between leaders and managers. Leaders focus on the future. They know what they want to accomplish; they can see five years into the future. To conceptualize this, they work from the future back to the present to show others how to get to the fulfillment of their vision.

Managers just don't see life that way. They conceptualize by working from the past to get to the present. They know how things used to operate. Now they build on the past to work efficiently in the present. They have no guidelines to take them into the future.

Let's see how this works on a practical level. Let's say we decide that we're going to have a banquet to honor our pastor's ten years of service to our congregation.

If you are a gifted manager, you will ask, "How did you do this before? What did you do on his fifth anniversary as pastor?" Or the manager might go to the files and church archives to find out how the church did it for the previous pastor who served almost thirty years. The managers will soon know exactly what time and what activities occurred. They'll know who spoke, where they held the banquet, how much they charged members, and even have a copy of the menu. Managers know the past, so they can tweak it to make it flow with the present.

If we're managers, we pride ourselves on being practical. If we're leaders, we pride ourselves on being imaginative and visionary.

If we give the same task to a leader, that person will start at a different place. "Forget five years ago. This is now. What's the purpose of this event? What do we want to see accomplished? What is the outcome we want from this banquet?"

Leaders will also ask, "Is this the best time to do this? Who do we need to call in to help us make this happen?"

Once they've established where they want to be at the end of the banquet, they work backward.

Here's another way of understanding leaders. They embrace a macro-perspective or the big picture; managers embrace a micro-perspective or a snapshot. It's difficult for managers to see anything that isn't on their desk. They focus on narrow, specific tasks—that's why they're good managers.

If we switch managers into leaders' roles every-thing stalls. If we try to make leaders into managers, they can't take their eyes off the skies long enough to figure how to strengthen the ladder or position all the people they need.

Leaders need to understand—especially those at the CEO or senior pastor level—that one of the great-est challenges they are going to continue to face is painting the large picture.

Leaders focus on the future. They work from the future back to the present to show others how to get to the fulfillment of their vision.

Managers conceptualize by working from the past to get to the present. They build on the past to work efficiently in the present.

They also know that when others may stare ahead, they don't always grasp what the leader sees. Others may say, "Okay, there's one house on the prairie. Yes, that's nice." The leader wants them to grasp the larger canvas that also includes mountains in the background and streams in the foreground. Leaders may want people to see the cumu-lous clouds that drift across the landscape, but viewers see only the glint of the sun's rays on the gentle-flowing stream.

Leaders understand that. In fact, with the help of managers, they form groups of stream gazers and house viewers. They themselves, however, continue to take in the large, over-all picture they've painted.

Leaders favor innovative thinking; they're full of

new ideas. They constantly push the boundaries, eager to try new programs or envision exciting opportunities.

Managers favor routine thinking. They want to know exactly what's expected of them and they'll do it faithfully. "You want me to hold the left side of this huge ladder?" they ask. "You bet! And no one will ever grip it more firmly than I will."

Managers don't have many original ideas. Leaders have a revolutionary flair and constantly turn things over, around, and upside down. Managers protect the status quo and they hold on. Change is difficult for managers. If you have put somebody in a department where you want to bring about change and improvement,

> *If we switch managers into leaders' roles everything stalls. If we try to make leaders into managers, they can't take their eyes off the skies long enough to figure how to strengthen the ladder or position all the people they need.*

and you put a manager over there, you cannot expect those things to happen because they're going to maintain the present status—perhaps more efficiently—but they won't transform the atmosphere.

As I've already pointed out, for leaders, the emphasis is on *what* and *why*; for managers the emphasis is *how* and *when*. Someone has said it this way: Those who know *how* will always work for those who know why.

Leaders inspire, and they're quick to challenge

and urge people to try new things. Managers control; they direct attention and activities. If we could see this as God's plan for church growth and that God needs both types, it could bring a lot of harmony into the way we put up and guard our ladders.

We need both. I often think that when we talk about leadership we make managers come across as less significant. One of the best purposes I see in

> **Those who know how will always work for those who know why.**

managers is that sometimes they are the ones who keep the painter's feet solidly on the ladder. Some visionaries are so caught up in their vision, they think they can walk on air or leap from building to building. Managers remind them of their human limitations.

Managers also guard tradition—and all tradition isn't bad. Many times the tradition is the framework, the solid foundation that we can never abandon if we want to keep our feet on the solid rock. We have only to think of leaders who have reached magnificent heights and then fallen to the ground; or they hung on helplessly until someone rescued them and got them started again.

On a personal level, I'm one of those visionary types, but God has given me a team with some managers. They remind me I'm earthbound when I want to fly into outer space. I'm also smart enough to listen to them. At times, I've also had to push them. On several occasions, they had reservations, but they trusted me and my vision. That's how God wants it to work, isn't it?

Let's see how this works in the church. Let's say Dr. Holmes, the CEO-pastor has a powerful vision for a big building going up. That's inspiring but unless he has controls in place he'll constantly be over budget and over time. Dr. Holmes started off with the sanctuary that would cost two million dollars, but his vision kept getting larger. He kept chang-

> *Change excites leaders and it frightens managers. We need both. Healthy fear is an ally.*

ing, seeing more efficient ways to reach larger numbers of people, to train more effectively, and to guide more troubled souls into the kingdom. His final vision is for a nine-building complex that will cost eighty million dollars. Everything will be in chaos unless a good manager brings in stability and control.

It's also true that change excites leaders and it frightens managers. We need both in an enterprise like that. Healthy fear is an ally.

Whenever we talk about modifications or adjustments, here's an important fact to remember: The one who proposes those changes is not the same as the person who is listening to the plans. If we put them both on a page, we'd have a line down the middle and they would be in two different columns.

If we draw a line through the middle of the page, the left-side column would be what I call the gain column; the right-hand column is what I call the loss column. When Pastor Holmes speaks to people and tells them about the changes, he's talking about the gain column. He emphasizes the good things that will come out of his ideas and projects. He won't tell them about the possibilities of failure or create doubts in their minds.

However, suppose single parent, Minnie Thomas, is listening. She can only think of the losses. The warmth and closeness of members will be gone. She used to be able to make appointments to talk to Bishop Holmes, but she won't be able to do that. He says they'll have a full time counselor, but Minnie Thomas wants the bishop.

> **Leaders identify opportunities; managers identify obstacles.**

Behind her sits Elder Kenny Sams. He's been a member of that church for fifty-one years. He was baptized there at age sixteen. Tears fill his eyes when he realizes that the old baptismal tank will be gone. He and his wife were married there and his wife's funeral was held in that building. Now all of that will be gone.

Dr. Holmes's business manager, Ezra Bird, currently has a corner office, but he knows from the new building plans that he'll now be stuck in an office with two windows that face another building. He also knows that his new office will measure six square feet less than his previous one. He's not excited about the change. He can see only loss.

When we talk about church growth we're talking about gain, but as the church grows, those who are actively involved may easily view that as a loss. Their influence, power, and control are eroded. Individuals with greater talents, stronger motivation, and more expertise will come in. Leaders need to understand that when they want to make things differ-

Leaders take risks; managers avoid risks.

ent. They themselves are excited about change but managers are threatened. Leaders move quickly; managers move slowly.

Here's another way to look at this. Leaders identify opportunities; managers identify obstacles. So in a business meeting, Dr. Holmes excitedly tells of the new building and how much more helpful they can be to the community and the influence they can have in human lives.

"But what about building permits?" Ezra Bird asks. "Have you thought of the property we're going to have to buy in this neighborhood? What happens if we can't make our budget next month? Remember, we barely paid our bills two months ago."

Leaders take risks; managers avoid risks.

As a leader, I've learned two things about this.

1. The larger risk is to refuse to take a risk. Nothing happens without taking risks.

2. If we wait until we're 100 percent sure, we're already too late.

As a wise person once said about baseball, "You can't steal second and still keep your foot on first."

For growth to happen, someone must take a risk. A leader pursues acquiring resources, but available resources limit managers. This means that if I am a leader and don't have the money, I can find some way to raise it. If I'm a manager, I'll say, "We do not have the money in the bank." Leaders see the empty coffers and know they can fill them; managers see only that the coffers are empty.

MAKING DECISIONS

I want to point out how most congregations make decisions. This is normally done in a board meeting, business meeting, session, or elders' meeting. The pastor has an excellent idea of how they can grow and increase their influence in the community. He presents his ideas and then he pauses and asks the treasurer or financial secretary, "Do we have the money?"

1. The larger risk is to refuse to take a risk.
2. If we wait until we're 100 percent sure, we're already too late.

I've learned that treasurers have been trained to move their heads only one way—and that is to say no. That's usually the death knell of moving ahead.

This all-too-frequent scenario means that the visionaries have allowed the nearsighted to make decisions about the future. They throw veto power into the hands of the status quo before the idea has had full discussion.

By contrast, shortly after I became president of Beulah Heights Bible College, I saw this working flawlessly. I began to make changes in how we made decisions because the school was facing serious difficulties. We had an enrollment of eighty seven students, the college was not accredited, and our staff was small, overworked, and underpaid.

Leaders see the empty coffers and know they can fill them; managers see only that the coffers are empty.

We had to take some risks. We had to think differently. I proposed a simple rule. We have four questions we need to ask before we make our decisions—and those four must be in the right order. As president, I could enforce this—and I did.

(1.) *Does this go along with our vision, mission, and core values?* Another way to ask is this: Is it something we are supposed to do? Not every Bible college, church, or organization is supposed to do everything. In fact, the fewer things an organization does, the better off they are because they can focus and do all of them well.

For example, is a ministry to the homeless a vibrant vital opportunity for God's church to express compassion? Yes, it is.

Is it part of our church's ministry? Maybe not.

Is reaching out to the refugees from Somalia a good thing to do? Absolutely, but it may not be part of the ministry that God has given us.

Are after-school tutoring and GED completion good things for a church to be involved in? Yes, but such educational programs may not be for us.

We can, however, resource those for whom it is †

their passion and challenge.

What we as a church, a Bible school, a para-church group must do is to answer this question: Is this going to be part of our vision and mission? Does it flow with our core values? Are we considering this only because it's a good program that's successful somewhere else?

2. *Do we have the heart to make this happen?* After all the discussion ends, it's going to take the heart—the zeal, the commitment—to make anything happen. Another way to put it for the business community is: Do we have the organizational capacity to make this a reality?

3. *How will God be glorified?* Not if God will be glorified, because we can say yes to almost all the opportunities that come our way. We're Christians and we sense needs or perceive opportunities. So our question is *how*? We want to be able to say that if we hold this conference, here are three ways that God will be glorified. We answer the question by saying, "Here are three ways we will glorify God if we expand our curriculum."

4. *How much will it cost?* We don't discuss money until we've answered the first three questions. No one can bring up the cost factor unless we have positive answers to the first three.

Part of the rule we adopted was that we don't ask, "Do we have the money?" If we have answered the first three questions and still believe this is for us, then we move ahead. Part of that moving ahead is figuring out what it will cost.

I've reminded the staff several times, "Salvation is free, but ministry is expensive." Once we know all those answers, we can begin to ask God to show us how to raise the money to do the ministry. This differs from starting with whether we have the funds. In many churches, and certainly at Beulah Heights, if we asked whether we had the money as our first question, by now our doors probably would have been closed. As of 2003, we are the fastest growing, predominately African-American Bible College in America. I believe it's because we're asking the correct questions and in the right order.

Here's another difference: Leaders are willing to say, "Let's acquire resources." Managers stop the discussion with, "But we don't have the resources."

Here are other differences: Leaders are people-centered and managers are system-centered. It's important for managers to have policies and procedures manuals. Leaders hate policies and procedures manuals, managers love them. That is why we attend a church conference and the managers quote the bylaws better than they do the Bible. They like systems. In fact, managers feel that if they can look at an organizational chart and move boxes across from one spot to another, they can transform the organization. We can move boxes all day long without effective results. Organizational charts don't contribute to the success of the corporation; people do.

It's like the question, "Do you want cancer in your right shoulder or your left?" We can move an inefficient individual (whose bad performance acts like a cancer) from one department to another. The people in the new division ask, "What did we do to deserve this?"

Here's yet another way to see this: Leaders are idea-centered and managers are plan-centered. That's a big difference because leaders say, "Here's what I'd like to do."

"I need a plan before I can do this," managers answer.

That is where fighting the battles between the two become inevitable. If they come out successful, it is because smart managers have taken the good ideas and said, "Okay, here's the plan on how we can bring this about." The best ladder holders are excellent man-agers. Once they devise a plan, they can make things happen.

> *For leaders, people's approval is a want; for managers, approval is a need.*

Leaders can talk leadership language and managers' language. Managers can talk only managers' language. That makes it incumbent on leaders to build a bridge, walk across it, and shake hands with managers.

Finally, for leaders, people's approval is a *want*; for managers, approval is a *need.*

If I were speaking to a group, I'd say at this point, "As a leader, I want you to approve of me." Those who say they don't care what people think are lying. In fact, people who go around saying, 'I don't care what people say,' probably care the most, or they wouldn't think about others' opinions. As a leader, however, I also know that I don't need someone's good opinion for me to function.

"I would like you to approve of me." I don't actually say those words, but approval is something I would like to have. When I speak at a conference or a banquet, I want to do a good job and want people to like what I say and to agree with my message. But it's still a want.

In almost any situation when I propose plans for growth, not everyone will like my message; a few people might strongly disagree. If people disagree or disapprove, that will concern me. I might think about it quite a bit. I might pray that the situation would change. Regardless, the disapproval of others wouldn't stop my going forward with my ideas. The disapproval of some wouldn't stop me from speaking to another group tomorrow on the same topic. Yes, I want approval but I don't need it.

Managers' need for approval means they have to be recognized by leaders. That puts a burden on leaders to understand and to keep managers' tanks filled. They can do that by simple affirmations. They can send e-mails, speak a few words of "Well done," or mail a thank you note. They can poke their heads into a manager's office and say, "The choir did great yesterday. Thanks for your hard work." Managers constantly need to be appreciated, valued, and affirmed.

When I was a pastor, I had to be a self-motivator and a self-starter. In fact I had to start in the face of all kinds of odds and get my tank filled in other ways than by having people come in and affirm me. The manager can only start if somebody else fills the tank.

For leaders, ideas, concepts, visions, dreams, and entrepreneurship fills their tank, puts a smile on their faces, and makes them excited. For managers, fulfillment, affirmation, and encouragement are the major motivators. They are always working for somebody else and they still have a need to feel significant because significance never goes away.

> **For leaders, ideas, concepts, visions, dreams, and entrepreneurship fills their tank, puts a smile on their faces, and makes them excited. For managers, fulfillment, affirmation, and encouragement are the major motivators.**

I'm the president of Beulah Heights Bible College and everybody else on staff is my ladder holder. I get my tank filled all over the country, "You're doing a great job." People don't usually call my dean and tell him what an outstanding job the college is doing. They say those words to me. They don't call my director of finance and say, "You ended in the black, you're doing great, you balanced the budget." No, they say those things to me.

Leaders are responsible to fill managers' tanks but managers don't fill leaders' tanks. In fact, leaders get into problems when they expect others to fill their tanks.

Haven't we all heard, "It's lonely at the top"?

We've heard those words, but I don't believe that. It's not lonely at the top. If those at the top are lonely, it's because they didn't take anybody up there with them. It doesn't have to be lonely, because there are other ladders there—right next to

> *Managers get the most out of themselves, but leaders get the most out of others.*

them. Those at the top of their ladders are doing what makes them happy. They can enjoy each other.

Finally, managers get the most out of themselves, but leaders get the most out of others. Leaders, by their nature, constantly lead and at the same time, they inspire others. They're the cheerleaders and encouragers and enable others to say, "Yes! Yes! I can do that!"

In *Catalyst* magazine for April 2003, Ben Dyer wrote an editorial that starts the article with these words: "If it weren't for the people involved, this would be an easy business." [4] Then he quotes John Imlay, a now-prominent investor who led the software company Mandrin Sciences of America. Imlay said, "People are the key." [5]

That's what this book is about—people are the key.

The new prospective owner of the Atlanta Thrashers and Atlanta Hawks, David McDavid, gave an interview to the *Atlanta Journal Constitution* on May 2, 2003, that became a headline article for the sport's section. He spoke about growing up around horses and added, "And that's not unlike sports teams by the way. You've got to have the personnel if you want to win." [6] In the same article, McDavid said, "But as an owner…I think my job would be to find the best general manager available… If I [were] going to try to make those decisions myself, I wouldn't need a general manager. But the fact is, I'm not competent to do that." A man of that caliber realized that his first job is to hire the best general manager and not to try to do that himself.

Can We Turn Ladder Holders into Ladder Climbers?

"Where did you start your climb upward?"

That's the question I'd like to ask every church and business leader. I'd like to know if they spotted a ladder, raced to it, and climbed to the top. Did they wait until someone waved them over and said, "Up you go"?

As I look at my own experience and consider the upward path of others, I suspect that most of them started at the bottom. That is, their careers began after they learned to hold the ladder securely for someone else to move smoothly upward.

They did more than hold the ladder. They observed, they learned, they saw the techniques used, and they understood where the ascending person was going. The day came when those same people who held ladders started their own climb upward.

That's not the end of the story either—at least not for the kind of leaders God calls into prominence in the church today. It's not enough for me to be at the top of the Beulah Heights Bible College ladder. I have another responsibility. God wants me to teach and empower others so they can

> **The only time you start at the top is when you're digging a hole.**

move from the role of supporters to climbers. Wouldn't it be a shame if we left ladder holders forever on the same job and they never did anything else?

God has blessed me with leadership ability. If I had stayed at the bottom and held everybody's ladder, would that have been the best use of my divinely given talents?

Of course not.

Those of us in leadership positions remember—or I hope we do—where we started. At one time I was the janitor, breakfast cook, and dishwasher at Beulah Heights. I held ladders so that others could succeed and minister.

Every effective business leader and every senior

pastor started somewhere. They may have already had the gifts that eventually pushed them up the ladder, but most of them didn't start there. God's plan was already in place but it started in a lowly ✝ position.

This is the biblical way. We read about Elisha, a man about whom the Bible records twice as many miracles as that of his mentor Elijah. But where did Elisha start? He held the ladder of the great prophet of Israel and faithfully followed until his turn came.

At one time I was the janitor, breakfast cook, and dishwasher at Beulah Heights. I held ladders so that others could succeed and minister.

Jesus called twelve disciples. He planned great ministries for each of them. From the beginning, He knew that one day He'd climb the ladder that would take Him all the way to heaven. He didn't leave the ladder empty, but chose those with potential to become expert ladder climbers.

We're here today because Jesus saved us, of course. But we're also here today because His disciples started as supporters for Jesus until their times came to move upward. They are the ones who continued the work after Jesus was ascended.

For example, I was born in India. Part of the reason I am in the United States today and involved in ministry is because of the faithfulness of one of the twelve—the apostle Thomas. As part of his ministry of going into all the world, he carried the gospel to my country and faithfully chose others to hold his ladder until his time came to leave this life. Thomas led others who then passed on the message through the centuries. I'm one of the modern beneficiaries of Thomas's faithfulness.

All of this is to say that we need to plan so that we turn ladder holders into ladder climbers. Otherwise, this becomes a self-serving club. I recruit a person to hold my ladder and say, "Now you stay there. You're not worthy of following my steps." Isn't it better to say, "This is where you are today, but this is not where God wants you to stay"? I can even add, "One day you'll climb your own ladder and you'll recruit those to support you while they grasp the first lessons of moving upward."

The need to train seems obvious, but I want to point out three things we need to do to ensure that we reach out and clasp the hands of others and help them take the first steps.

STEPS FOR TURNING LADDER HOLDERS INTO LADDER CLIMBERS

The first step is what I call *spiritual formation of a leader.* In this spiritual formation we deal with security issues, finding purpose, and our destiny. At the age of forty-four, I finally discovered who I was and what I was called to do.

I discovered that my primary motivation is to help others succeed. In fact, I have that statement written on the home page of my website (www.samchand.com or www.dreamreleaser.org)

and it reads: Samuel R. Chand Ministries, Inc. is an enhancing and collaborative process in developing leaders who in turn reproduce more leaders.

As I pondered that statement, I realized that I loved doing leadership development and it feeds my passion. It brought me fulfillment at a deeper level. As clearly as I perceived who I am, it was just as clear who I am not and what I don't want to do. I am someone who is motivated by the opportunity to develop leaders.

As I've grappled with leadership development, it occurred to me that we talk a lot about near-death experiences. I'm convinced that most people have what I call near-life experiences. They come close to being fully alive but never discover who they really are. They never work passionately at the things they're good at doing. Until we discover who we are, we won't climb the steps of the ladder that God wants us to climb.

We want to help people develop who they are. We want them to be able to answer these questions:

- What am I passionate about?
- What are my gifts and talents?
- To what kind of work is God calling me?
- What frustrates me?
- What makes me cry?
- What brings me joy?

If we can tune into those things, those existential concepts in lives, we're going to get the best results and place people in the right places.

My second step is *skill formation*. I was greatly

challenged when I read the book, *The Four Obsessions of an Extraordinary Executive* by Patrick Lencioni. Written as a parable, Lencioni tells the story about two companies that flourished. One of them grew and the people were happy and healthy. The second succeeded by cutting corners. Even though outwardly successful, the people in the second company were never as happy as those in the first. In the healthier-happier company, people knew who they were and what they were doing. They understood the soul of their company.

That book so challenged me I went to work to discover the soul of Beulah Heights Bible College. It took time and effort on my part, but I figured out the answer. In doing so, I also learned how to keep people aware of our five core values.

If anyone walks onto our campus today, they'll see posters with those concepts displayed—in every office, every classroom, every hallway, and even in every restroom. We have a five-color poster called "The Soul of Beulah Heights Bible College." On that poster we list our vision, our mission, our core values, and our theme.

The Soul of
Beulah Heights Bible College

Our Vision

Academic Excellence
Resource Center
Change Agent

Our Mission

BHBC develops relevant Christian leaders for ministry and marketplace.

Our Core Values

Biblical Inerrancy
Integrity
Global Missions
Dedicated Servanthood
Diversity

Our Theme

Breaking the Mold –
Bridging the Gap!

For more information: (404) 627-2681 / Fax (404) 627-0702
892 Berne St. S.E. / P.O. Box 18145 / Atlanta, GA 30316 • www.beulah.org

I'm not naïve enough to think that just putting up posters does the job. I use them as constant reminders. I want to use whatever methods I can to promote the soul of Beulah Heights and to inculcate our values into our own souls. I do this based on a simple principle: *What we do must flow out of who we are.*

> **In most churches we train but we don't develop.**

By contrast, in most churches we train but we don't develop.

Training carries a specific, narrow focus; developing is a broad focus.

- Training is task-centered; development is people-centered.
- Training is about a job as an usher, as a deacon, as a Sunday school teacher; development involves the whole person.

After we know who we are, *what* we do will always be a project. For example, in 2003 we had twenty-seven countries represented on our campus, so we promoted an International Day. We made it a big event. People wore their national regalia, presented their music, spoke their languages, and allowed us to sample their food.

When I addressed those present, I said, "Today is not a program. Today is not an international day program. This is who we are."

I wanted to affirm them, celebrate our differences, and enable all of us to pull together. This is two of our five core values. Global missions is a core value, diversity is a core value. This is who we are. So this is not a program, this is us. In churches we often do not take people beyond the tasks to really develop them spiritually, and that is why people ✝ come and people go but they don't take roots.

Rick Warren's book, *The Purpose-Driven Church*, helped me understand how this works. He uses the concept of baseball.

First base is salvation where *spiritual formation* begins. Here the focus is on spiritual discipline and developing us as individuals.

Second base would be what I call *skill formation*. This is where we change and begin to focus on others. We're trained to do ministry through our local church.

Third base is *strategic formation*. Here we focus on extending God's kingdom on earth and on leadership development. This refers to ministry to the church at large. We can be members of one church but have a heart for helping the

> **It's more difficult to unlearn than it is to learn.**

homeless. Our church doesn't have a ministry to those needy people, but we remain members and involve ourselves in a para-church ministry to the ✝ homeless.

That is what happens when we're not confined to ministry exclusively within the walls of our local building. We're developing our vision and focusing on global outreach.

To continue the baseball analogy, we can sometimes

reach third base, but we don't win games by staying there. We have to make it to home plate. That is when we develop other leaders. For ladder climbers, bringing someone home is when we turn our ladder *holders* into our ladder *climbers*.

UNLEARNING AND LEARNING

In developing leadership skills, I've learned that it's more difficult to *unlearn* than it is to *learn*.

My experience with golf may help explain this. Years ago when I lived in Oregon a friend said, "Let's play golf."

"Yes, let's do that." I had never played golf before, but my friend was fairly good at the game. I enjoyed his company and figured there wasn't too much to learn to play golf.

A few days before we played, I stopped by a yard sale and bought an old set of clubs and went out to the range. I felt highly confident because I had everything I needed. I put my baseball grip on my club and started hacking. Over a period of months, I became a pretty good hacker.

When I moved to Atlanta, friends invited me to golf with them. I agreed to play but after a few games, I realized that I was stretching my relationship. I was a hacker and they were golfers.

One day a friend shook his head after I took six tries to get my ball about a hundred yards. "How do you hold your club?" he asked.

I showed him. I held my club like a baseball bat.

He showed me how I needed to change my grip by entwining my fingers. "Oh that looks easy," I said.

Yes, it looked easy, but I couldn't get it. No matter how hard I tried to unlearn my old grip, I just couldn't get away from it. I had been holding my fingers that way too long. It's been more than

> *The best use of power is to give it away. We give it away by investing in others.*

ten years since I tried to unlearn how to hold a golf club. I have never tried golf again. I just could not unlearn.

Here's one more way I realized the problem of unlearning. While I was a pastor in Michigan, I preached a sermon about obeying God's calling on our lives. Eleven people came forward for the altar call. Among them were our organist, pianist, bass guitarist, and drummer. Two weeks later, all of them left the church to enter Beulah Heights Bible College.

That left me without musicians. I decided I would learn to play the piano. I have a good ear and I already had learned to play several songs in C, F, and G. Years earlier I had learned to play in what I called honky-tonk style. I got the job done as church musician, but I wasn't good, and I didn't know how to become a "real" musician.

Even today I still play honky-tonk style and can play almost any song people want to sing, I've learned a few techniques since then, but my style is still country style with a lot of chords. If a good music teacher tried to show me how to do runs (and they have tried), how to use the entire keyboard, or to expand my reach, I'd have to unlearn my fingering pattern to do that. I've been playing country style too long to unlearn.

Church leaders can save themselves a lot of heartache if they think carefully about those who join them after having been long-time members of another congregation. It's a big challenge for them to unlearn the way things were done in their previous church and to learn how it's done in the new.

By strategic formation we refer to plans for developing other ladder holders.

I wonder what it would be like if I visited Joyful Praise Church next Sunday. Let's say I came inside, listened to a powerful message, the Holy Spirit convicted me of sin, and I raised my hand when the pastor extended an invitation for salvation. I walked down the aisle and someone led me to a backroom, prayed with me, and taught me how to surrender my life to the Lord.

> *Most of the leaders of my generation—the boomer generation—are accidental leaders. We stumbled into leadership.*

"What happens next?" I asked.

"Joyful Praise has a new converts' class."

That's good. Or perhaps it's a new members' class. That's good. I spend four or ten weeks learning. That's good.

"What happens after that?"

"Just swim with the sharks. Make it the best way

that you can." No one would actually say those words, but that's the unspoken message I'd probably receive.

So what happens next?

Most church leaders don't know. That's not good.

It could be good if we changed the way it was done. After someone took me into the back room and helped me understand the first steps of faith, then the person says to me, "Sam, for the next few weeks we're going to invest ourselves in your spiritual ⊥ development."

I may not be clear about what that means, but I realize that I'm being trained as an individual. Teachers and guides will take me from first base to second (skill formation), and I'll stay there until I'm ready to move on to third base.

> *We need to get the right people on the bus and get the wrong people off. Then we need to get the right people in the right seats on the bus.*

"We're going to move you into strategic formation (third base)," says the senior pastor months after my conversion. "Our purpose is not for you to be a good church member here. Our purpose is that one day you'll be doing what I'm doing right now. It won't necessarily be pastoring a church but you'll be developing other leaders. We recognize your leadership gifts and we want to help you devel- ✝ op them."

How many congregations operate like that?

Not many.

I'm suggesting that we strive for a holistic system to turn ladder holders into ladder climbers. We need to empower them and give them permission to climb upward. I've learned that the best use of power is to give it away. We give it away by investing in others.

This isn't everyone. Not everyone is a leader. There will always be people who love holding ladders and who have no desire to ascend the heights. That's fine—if that's their choice.

Most of the leaders of my generation—the boomer generation—are *accidental leaders.* We stumbled into leadership. I don't remember anybody ever saying to me, "Sam, I see some potential in you."

People sent me signals, but no one said, "I'd like to walk this journey with you. You don't have to call me mentor. Here's my phone number. Call me any time. In fact, if you don't mind, may I keep tabs with you and watch how you're doing?"

I wish someone had done that; so do many other accidental leaders. I've proven this many times in conferences and meetings. "How many of you had somebody who intentionally developed you? someone who took you under his or her wing?" In early 2003, I asked a group of 300 pastors in Cincinnati.

One man raised his hand. *Just one.*

Here's the challenge. We can only give what we have. We can't pass on what we don't possess, because most of us teach the way we were taught. Are we going to inflict the same accidental leadership on the next generation? Or are we going to have a plan?

The new generation that's already filing into our churches wants to know where we're going. In the past, we may have been happy to go to church Sunday morning, midweek service, and enroll in the choir. Not so with this generation. They want to know if there is more.

This is just as true in the business world. Those same people join the organization at the entry level, but most of them don't want to stay there. If they're eagles, they want to fly. If they're ladder climbers, they don't want to stay on the ground.

> *"If he were a nonbeliever or a pagan, you could fire him and he'd still be your friend."*

As soon as they hit the ceiling—at whatever level— and realize the ladder they're on won't go any higher, they'll leave. They'll go to corporations with higher ceilings.

Jim Collins's bestseller *Good To Great* helped me understand this. He used the idea of getting the right people on the bus and getting the wrong people off. Then we need to get the right people in the right seats on the bus.

The first two things are pretty obvious—getting good people on the bus and getting rid of those who don't belong. The third part gives us heartaches because once people get on the bus, we're not always sure what to do with them.

Collins's concept made me aware of one of the most excruciating years of my life. At Beulah Heights, I recognized that a person who had held my twenty-foot ladder did an excellent job—as long as I used that same ladder. When I decided to climb a forty, foot ladder he couldn't hold it for me. The person who does an excellent job of holding a twenty-foot ladder may not be the same person we need if we want to go higher.

It caused me intense pain to realize that good people—committed, hard working individuals and people of integrity—may not be the ones we need to help us move on to the next level.

How do we respectfully disengage them from our organization and how do we respectfully bring in or promote from within someone who was holding a six-foot ladder and put that person in charge of forty-foot ladder holders? That means bypassing the twenty-foot holders or moving them out of their positions. That's never easy.

I remember having a conversation with one of my mentors in the business community. I asked, "Have you ever fired a friend?"

"Yes."

"Can you help me put together a plan in which I can fire this friend and still keep him as my friend?"

He smiled and asked, "Is he a Christian?"

"Absolutely. He's a dedicated, committed—Christian."

"You can't do it then. If he were a nonbeliever or a pagan, you could fire him and he'd still be your friend."

I stared at him and wondered how that could be. As I pondered his answer, I knew he was right. In the church, that's the challenge of leadership and a painful thing to realize.

Let's say I'm the pastor of a church with one hundred members. Marian is my secretary and she's a dedicated worker and has been in that position since 1980. She can type fast, and back in the 1980s and early 1990s she spent many hours fighting with an inky mimeograph machine to put out a church bulletin every week. No matter what the task, all of us could depend on Marian. Many nights she stayed until long after dark and came in on Saturdays. No task was too big or too small for Marian.

The years passed and we entered a new century and the church now has a thousand members. Marian was a wonderful, faithful, dependable ladder holder then. She isn't today.

She never could figure out the computer. She uses it, of course, but she hates it. She can't understand why we don't keep using the mimeograph because it's cheaper than running off bulletins on the laser printer. Spreadsheets confuse her and only reluctantly does she use e-mail to communicate with members.

What happens now? Do we spare Marian's feelings and work around her? Do we fire her? Demote her by asking her to become the receptionist and answer the telephone? She was absolutely the best ladder holder when our ladder only reached twelve feet, but she can't handle one that rises to fifty feet. Should we keep seeking another twelve-foot ladder so we can make Marian happy?

Most growing organizations don't have another twelve-foot ladder, so people like Marian have maxed out. In a corporation, because we know they have hit their ceiling, we don't want to transfer a maxed-out worker from one department to the other. Such workers have chosen to remain at the their current level and refuse to learn new skills in order to move ahead.

In a corporation, the secretary would know there would be a forty-foot ladder coming up. She could preserve her job by learning the skills needed for the larger task. But what if she refuses? What if she chooses to retain her skill level where she is? Or if she increases her skills only when forced to learn more?

By contrast, let's say Hulda is the technology person and has spent a lot of time to learn our information system. She understands our software and can do programming, and she can run everything and figure out all the bugs in the new systems. Our company now begins to expand because we're making more sales. We have more sales people out there. Customers are buying from us off the web. Hulda has proven herself invaluable to the corporation and she'll move ahead.

What about people like Marian who refuse to keep progressing? They have chosen to become obsolete. That may sound harsh, but it's true.

This presents a great dilemma in leadership and is one of the most difficult tasks. As the leader, I have to look at Marian. Even though I admire her

Page 98   Who's Holding Your Ladder?

and value her years of service, I also admit that she is holding up the progress of the church. Eventually, I will have to fire her. Thirty-year-old Hulda has been with the company only two years, but she will replace the fifty-three-year-old who has been a long-time employee, but has stayed at the same skill level for the past twenty-years.

In a business, people understand that their skills have not kept up with the demands. They may resent being fired, but they understand. In the church, however-

"Old leaders are rarely new leaders."

er, we have a different scenario. "I love the Lord. I work harder than anyone else," they wail. "No one is more committed to service than I am."

No matter how I may try to reason with her, Marian probably won't face the reality that she isn't able to work with anything more than a twelve-foot ladder. She can't understand why we no longer need short ladders.

We need different ladder holders for different levels in the organization. Old leaders are rarely new leaders because people continue to view the organization at the level they came to it, where as new leaders see it as it is now.

For example, a church leader who joined the church when it was 100 members will have a difficult time leading the church when it is 1000 members, because he still thinks of the church as it "used to be."

So what do we do?

Are We Looking up the Ladder?

Several times I have wrestled with the issue of how to handle people who refuse to grow with the organization. One of the most helpful things I did was to consult other leaders. How did they handle such situations?

A quote from Ken Blanchard helped me immensely. He came into prominence in the late 1970s when he co-wrote *The One Minute Manager*. In a written interview by Patricia Baldwin in *Private*

Clubs, Blanchard said:

> "...we're only as good as the person who's answering the phone, the person who's greeting the customers, the person who deals with complaints. Nobody cares who's the president of a company." [7]

He goes on to say, "If you create a great human organization, then everything else takes care of itself." [8]

In the previous chapter I mentioned that Patrick Lencioni's book *The Four Obsessions of an Extraordinary Executive* profoundly affected me. He started talking about the soul of the organization. I

> **"If you create a great human organization, then everything else takes care of itself."**

had signs called "The Soul of Beulah Heights Bible College" plastered all over the walls, but I knew that, by themselves, they wouldn't make any difference. I had to spend time with the ladder holders and help them see the significance of their roles. That way the signs would mean something—they would express their attitudes and values and not just mine.

In the first chapter of this book, I pointed out that if we opt to develop leaders it takes time. And it does!

After I thought about this a great deal, I asked my assistant to set me up half-hour appointments with everyone on the staff—full time and part time. When I met with them, I explained that this was not a job evaluation. Some might have their jobs changed but nobody was going to be dismissed.

When they came in I went over their job description and what they were doing for the college. I let them tell me about their job.

"What is your passion?" I asked. "Where do you find your greatest joy?"

One person said, "I hate what I'm doing."

"What would you love to do?"

She told me and we made changes. She is now doing the job she loves. Later she said, "Now I look forward to coming to work every day."

They were all good people and, to use Jim Collins's metaphor, they all belonged on the bus. We just didn't have everyone in the right seat. It was my fault as president that they didn't feel fulfilled or didn't like the ladder they had to hold. Out of those conversations, I made three changes by shifting personnel. At that time, I terminated no one.

The principle is simple. If people are joyful and love what they're doing, it will show in everything ✝ they do. When they answer the phone, the caller will know they're happy in their jobs.

I tell the people at the reception desk, "You are the director of first impressions." I know that before people meet the president, go into any of the classrooms, or listen to any of our great instructors, they will hear a voice on the telephone. They'll see that person as soon as they open the office door.

> *I tell the people at the reception desk, "You are the director of first impressions."*

We also needed to have curb appeal on our

campus. There's no litter on our grounds. No one will see paper cups on the ground or candy wrappers blowing in the wind. We want visitors to see a caring, efficient organization no matter where they look.

**

Another expert is Bernie Marcus, the co-founder and former CEO of The Home Depot. He said, "You have to know what you do best and do it. The notion that you can make it at anything you want to do just isn't true. There are things you can and can't be successful at. You have to sit down and measure your skills—strong and weak—and then build toward the strengths." [9]

> *"You have to know what you do best and do it. The notion that you can make it at anything you want to do just isn't true."*

The author points out that Marcus learned to focus after he had previously failed with another company. He built a home improvement colossus. "My strengths were as an entrepreneur and a merchant but not on the day-to-day. So I focused on those areas, as well as on people, *and surrounded myself with great operators.*" [10]

He was talking about ladder holders. He goes on to say, "You are only as good as the people around you. So surround yourself with good people" [11]

Paraphrasing his words, it means we can only go as high as the person holding the ladder lets us. Our height is controlled not by us but by the people on the ground level.

The president and chief operating officer of the Ritz-Carlton Hotel, Simon Cooper, said in an interview, "My challenge is how to continue the company's growth, based upon our founding principles. Therefore, I'm focused on both human and financial capital. After all, we're not going to be successful if we don't attract and retain the absolute best human capital as well as financial capital." [12]

Anyone who's ever stayed at a Ritz-Carlton knows the difference is not necessarily the rooms. We can get good rooms at other hotels as well. The difference is their service. They profile customers, know what they prefer, and provide for their comfort.

S. Truett Cathy, founder of Chick-fil-A, the fastest growing fast-food franchise in the world, gives his recipe for business success: "It requires a lot of time and effort to make sure you have the right people working the right jobs, but we believe it is time well spent. Customer satisfaction is the payoff." [13]

Another article written in the *Atlanta Journal Constitution* said that people skills are most important. They prefer attitude to aptitude. "Given a choice, Georgia employers say they'd take an adaptable 'people' person over a technically proficient worker." [14] This conclusion came from a survey conducted by the Metro Atlanta Chamber of Commerce in early 2003.

The first question to Leonard Roberts, president of Radio Shack, in an interview that appeared in Delta's *Sky* magazine, was: "What is the greatest challenge your industry faces?" [15]

Roberts is in a technical field, and I would have assumed he would refer to technical challenges or keeping up with the rapid growth in electronic breakthroughs. Here is his answer: "Our biggest challenge is making sure we have the right people on board, trained properly, and qualified to provide the answers Americans need about technology." [16]

> **"...If we don't get the people right...we lose everything."**

There it was again: people before technology.

Here is the last question and answer of that interview:

"What if it [strategy] goes wrong?"

"...If we don't get the people right, it all goes away. We lose everything."

Wayne Gretzky, who is recognized as the greatest ice hockey player in history, was asked, "What's the most important thing you've learned as a restaurateur?"

"That your partner's gotta know what he's doing. I have a great partner. He's been in the restaurant business with his family for more than 50 years. They know what they're doing. *The best thing you can do is make sure you pick the right people, and I've got a great partner.*" [17] (Emphasis mine.)

In an interview with Gerd H. Klauss, president and CEO of Volkswagen of America, the interviewer said: "The head of every major automobile company claims that his company is the best, but Volkswagen truly is a global trademark. What is it that makes the company so successful?" [18]

As part of his answer, Klauss said, "Volkswagen attracts people who are proud to be different, who ✝ don't always follow the mainstream." [19]

To put it in my language, Klauss refers to the kind of people we want to attract as ladder holders.

How Did Jesus Choose Ladder Holders?

"How *did* Jesus choose ladder holders?" I asked myself that question several times, and I think Luke 5:1-11 holds the answer. In that account, Luke records the incident where Peter, James, and John fished all night and caught nothing. After they have given up and were busily washing their nets, Jesus boarded one of the boats, taught the people, and then told Peter to go out and fish again.

Even though they who were professional fishermen

had caught nothing, Peter did what Jesus told him. To his amazement, they caught so many fish their nets broke and they had to ask other fishermen to help them.

The account ends when Jesus tells them that from now on they won't be catching fish. They'll be catching people. This story is recognized as Jesus calling three of His disciples.

Peter, James, and John were partners before Jesus called them. Jesus didn't break up their partnership.

Although I had read the passage many times, one day I noticed that Luke 5:10 refers to "James and John, the sons of Zebedee, which were partners with Simon [Peter]." This means they were partners before Jesus called them. Jesus didn't break up their partnership.

If we follow the life of Jesus, we see that He had just called His three major ladder holders. After that, everywhere He goes He always takes that trio with Him *as a group.* If they were partners in the fishing business, given the culture and the norms of that time it is fair to assume that their fathers and perhaps grandfathers had been partners.

Here's how Jesus operated with the three partners. One day He went to the house of Jairus. The man's daughter had died, and Jesus took the threesome with him. They were with Him at the Mount of Transfiguration. At the end of His journey when He prayed at Gethsemane, Jesus called all His disciples and then took the three men farther into the garden with Him.

This is the way the Lord worked. He first called a group of twelve. But even there, He chose individuals. In Luke 5:27-28, Luke records, "And after these things he went forth, and saw a publican, named Levi, sitting at the receipt of custom: and he said unto him, Follow me. And he left all, rose up, and followed him."

I also want to point out the word translated *saw* in this passage. It's the Greek *theaomai*. Although there are a dozen words in Greek for seeing, this word rarely appears. It carries the idea of seeing attentively—staring—and is sometimes translated as *to behold*. Scholars call it a solemn word and "is used for visionary seeing and the apprehension of higher realities." [20]

Although not a common word in the New Testament, *theaomai* has four distinct meanings. Each one stresses the action of the person who is seeing.

1. To observe with desire
2. To observe for a time
3. To spend time with
4. To look or study closely

Especially notice the fourth meaning. That's the point Luke makes in using *theaomai*. Jesus wasn't looking around casually. He scrutinized or focused carefully. It is as if Jesus gazed thoroughly into the man and then—and only then—did he say, "Follow me."

Jesus recruited Levi with a purpose in mind. All through the Gospels, Matthew is just one of the twelve, but Jesus had a special purpose for him. Levi, also known as Matthew, was someone who knew how to keep accurate records—that was his business as a tax collector. What the former tax collector didn't realize was that, even then, Jesus was preparing him to write an accurate account of events. It would be called the Gospel According to Matthew, the first book in the New Testament.

> **People are recruited as ladder holders as a group, but they continue as individuals.**

Jesus is still doing the same kind of *theaomai* today. He is gazing at us on two levels—our role as part of the group and as individuals.

Here's the point: People are recruited as ladder holders as a group, but they continue as individuals.

At Beulah Heights Bible College when I was going through that difficult time of dealing with personnel issues, people repeatedly asked each other three questions. (Of course, none of them asked me.)

1. Does Sam see what we see? Everyone in our office knew the weak links. They could see the incompetence. They didn't think of those individuals as bad people, but only as those who were unable to get the job done.

2. If Sam sees what we see, why doesn't he do something about it?

3. If Sam doesn't see what we see, what kind of leader is he?

Eventually I asked some people to leave the bus,

invited new ones inside, and changed the seating arrangements; we began to function more efficiently. That's when I learned about the three questions they had been asking each other.

After I made the changes, the people came to me with statements that started with one word: *finally.*

"Finally, somebody did something."

"Finally, somebody saw what we've known all along."

"Finally, somebody had the courage to make it happen."

Until then I didn't realize that they were questioning my leadership—and they were right to do so, because they saw the entire organization suffering from what they considered my inaction.

I did the right things; I just did some of them a little late.

Whose Ladder Are You Holding?

In reading what I've written so far, some may assume that if we're leaders, all we need to do is concentrate on and develop other ladder holders. That's only half the concept.

Here's the other half: Every true disciple of Jesus Christ holds somebody's ladder. That's God's plan. We need each other and we fulfill God's plan when we hold others' ladders.

We tend to forget that those of us who are leaders

are ladder climbers and also ladder holders. Furthermore, we'll always be ladder holders even if we're high-stepping climbers. Effective leaders understand that they are holding someone's ladder, whether it's the business-partner's ladder, that of another church pastor, or a denominational leader. God has called all of us to hold ladders for others.

> **God has called all of us to hold ladders for others.**

Effective leaders recognize two facts:

1. In leadership we will always need ladder holders.
2. In leadership we will also hold someone else's ladder. We are meant to support, assist, and help others in their climb upward.

Another way to get to this is to ask ourselves: What kind of ladder holder would I like? For example, earlier in this book, I wrote about needing ladder holders with five characteristics. They must be strong, attentive, faithful, firm, and loyal. Isn't it obvious that we need to be the kind of people we want others to become? If we want to develop superior ladder holders, we need to become superior ladder holders ourselves.

If you are a leader, here's my challenge to you: Whose ladder can you hold? What business leader can you mentor? Instead of looking at potential recruits and asking, "How can they serve me?" ask, "How can I serve them?"

God always intended for service to be a street

where we travel both ways. It is the law of reciprocity and it teaches us that what we give will come back to us. That's absolutely true; however, the problem is that we can only give what we have. We can only pass on what we possess. If we aren't good ladder holders, how can we expect to have good ladder holders helping us?

It makes me think of the law of tithing in the Old Testament. God required all faithful Jews to give 10 percent of their income to support the priests (hold their ladders). That's not the end

> *Even though we are ladder climbers, we're also ladder holders.*

of the law. The priests then gave ten percent to support the high priest. Even the priests had ladders to hold. That's always God's way of working.

If each of us is able to acknowledge the principle, it means that although we're leaders, we're also ladder holders. Here are a few more questions for us to ponder:

- Do I possess those five essential qualities of good ladder holders?
- Do I *intentionally* hold someone else's ladder?
- Am I a dependable ladder holder?
- When was the last time I walked past a visionary leader and said, "I really like his vision and like where he's going. I want to work alongside him and assist him by holding his ladder"?
- When was the last time I asked, "What leader can I help?" (Too often we are only looking for

people to help us.)

- What does it say about us if we always seek someone to hold our ladder, but we're unwilling to hold another person's ladder?

There's an old saying that most preachers will travel to the other corner of the world to preach a sermon, but they won't cross the street to hear one. Is that true of me? Here are other questions to ask ourselves:

- When was the last time I attended a leadership conference when I wasn't a speaker?
- When did I go to a conference just to hear somebody else?
- When was the last time I read a book and thought, I really like this, and then corresponded with the author?
- When was the last time I saw somebody else's advertisement in a magazine and said, "I want to serve that person"?

It's the principle, which is also in the Bible, that we reap what we sow. If we sow holding ladders, we reap those who will hold our ladders. We receive by giving. This is just as true with ladder holding as anything else.

> **What does it say about us if we always seek someone to hold our ladder, but we're unwilling to hold another person's ladder?**

It's not easy for many of us in leadership to be ladder holders, especially those of us, like me, who are accidental leaders.

I still remember the question my friend, Tom

Fortson, asked me. Tom, the executive vice president of Promise Keepers, visited Beulah Heights one day and I gave him a tour around the college. On the steps to our chapel he paused and asked, "Can you tell me when you became a leader?"

"No, I really can't," I said. Immediately my mind flashed back to something John Maxwell once told me about himself. If Tom Fortson had asked John when he became a leader, John would have known how to answer. For him, that defining moment happened during his elementary school days. The class planned a mock courtroom. The students chose the jury, the defendant, the defense attorney, and the prosecutor. The class elected John the judge. Because of their confi-

> *I'm an accidental leader, but I don't want to be an accidental mentor.*

dence in his ability, on that day, John knew he was going to become a leader.

I told that story to Tom Fortson and added, "I haven't had that kind of epiphany in my life. I've just been one of those to whom leadership was slowly revealed."

Tom's question has stayed with me and I've thought about it many times. When I speak in churches, I discover that most of the senior pastors are also accidental leaders. It's just as true when I ask about leadership in the marketplace.

I'm fifty years old at the time of writing this book. I can't recall a single instance during my time in Bible college, seminary, or denominational experience when anyone pointed out my leadership ability. Not once has a single person ever said to me, "I see potential in you. Good things are going to happen in your life. Could I walk with you? May I hold your ladder?"

Fine individuals have given me excellent advice; others have opened doors for me. No one has walked with me as my ladder holder. The realization that no one openly and intentionally mentored me has caused me to become more intentional to mentor others. That's my way of holding ladders.

> *As leaders, when we start upward, our most important decision is to choose the right ladder holders; as ladder holders, our most important decision is to select which ladders we hold.*

For some people, that ability flows freely and they simply do it. Because the ability comes naturally, they rarely think much about it. Others like me don't find it easy because we have no role model to guide us. Because I was never intentionally mentored, I don't know the tracks to run on. I'm an accidental leader, but I don't want to be an accidental mentor.

Here are some large and final questions:

- Whose ladder are you holding right now?
- Who is climbing upward and trusting you to be there at the bottom, bracing the ladder for him or her?
- Who is climbing high because you stepped out of the way and said, "Let me support you"?
- Who will look back one day and say, "I rose

forty-five feet in the air because you held my ladder"?

We have opportunities to be somebody's ladder holder. Because no one has done it for us, it may be difficult to intentionally commit ourselves to holding ladders, but it's not impossible. And it doesn't excuse us. It only means that it may take a little more effort for us accidental leaders to become intentional servants. But we can do it. We can commit ourselves to learning how to hold the ladders so others can climb high and some of them may even soar above us.

Nobody ever climbed Mt. Everest without a team. People climb Stone Mountain outside Atlanta because it's a relatively easy path and they don't need a team. No matter how high we go we should be holding somebody else's ladder—that's God's plan.

> *When we accomplish great things on our own ladder, we remember what we've done. When we intentionally hold others' ladders and they accomplish great things, they remember us. Their achievements become our legacy.*

As leaders, when we start upward, our most important decision is to choose the right ladder holders; as ladder holders, our most important decision is to select which ladders we hold.

Here's one way I like to think of it. When we accomplish great things on our own ladder, we remember what we've done. When we intentionally hold others' ladders and they accomplish great things, they remember us. Their achievements become our legacy.

Teaching This Material

You may find an opportunity to teach this material. I hope you will. To facilitate that, I have placed an outline of the material in this book on the pages that follow. Please feel free to copy the outline with the blanks as a handout. After that is a completed outline. This book puts flesh on that skeleton.

WHO IS HOLDING YOUR LADDER?

IN LEADERSHIP, THE MOST IMPORTANT DECISION YOU WILL MAKE IS S_____ YOUR LADDER HOLDERS.

1. Is someone holding your L_____?

2. What kind of P_____ is holding your ladder?

    A. Do you have to constantly R_____ them?

    B. Are they C_____ or intentional?

    C. Do they have their eye on Y_____ or are they looking around?

    D. Do they have a firm grip on your "ladder" or V_____?

3. Qualities of an effective ladder holder

    A. S_____

    B. A_____

    C. F_____

    D. F_____

    E. L_____

4. Ladder holders must be T_____.

    A. Very few ministers have Q_____
        and T_____ladder holders.

    B. Your armor bearer/A_____ may not
        necessarily be your ladder holder.

    C. People need C_____ instruction.

5. Ladder P_____ and perspective

    A. The greatest tragedy is to climb to the top of the
        ladder, only to find your ladder is leaning against the
        W_____ building.

    B. Assess

        (1) W_____ you want to go.

        (2) W_____ you're on the ladder.

        (3) W_____ tools you need up there—you
        can't keep going up and down.

6. Two basic categories of ladder holders

    A. L_____

    B. M_____

LEADERS	**MANAGERS**
Conceptualize outcome by	Conceptualize plans by work-
working from the	ing from the P_____ to
F_____ back to the	the P_____.
P_____.	Embrace a M_____
Embrace a M_____	perspective—snapshot
perspective—big picture	Favor R_____ thinking
Favor I_____ thinking	P_____ of the status
R_____ flair	quo
Emphasis on the	Emphasis on the
W_____ and	H_____ and
W_____	W_____
I_____ and motivating	C_____ and directing
E_____ by change	T_____ by change
Move Q_____	Move S_____
Identify O_____	Identify O_____
Take R_____	Avoid R_____
Pursue acquisition of	Actions limited by
R_____	A_____ resources
P_____ centered	S_____ centered
I_____ centered	P_____ centered
People's approval is a	People's approval is a
W_____	N_____

SUMMARY:

Managers get the most out of T_____. Leaders get the most out of O_____.

7. Turning ladder H_____into ladder C_____

    A. S_____ formation

        (1) Security issues

        (2) Finding purpose and destiny

    B. S_____ formation

        (1) Helping other ladder holders

        (2) Delegation

        (3) Communication

    C. S_____ formation

        (1) Plan for developing other ladder holders

        (2) Mentoring—See it (K_____); pursue it (G_____) and help others see it (S_____)

        (3) Empowering others

8. Whose ladder are Y_____ holding?

A. In leadership you will always need
   L_____ holders.

B. In leadership you will always hold someone else's
   L_____.

CONCLUSION:

IN LEADERSHIP, THE MOST IMPORTANT DECISION YOU
WILL MAKE IS SELECTING YOUR LADDER HOLDERS.

WHO IS HOLDING YOUR LADDER?

IN LEADERSHIP, THE MOST IMPORTANT DECISION YOU WILL MAKE IS **SELECTING** YOUR LADDER HOLDERS.

1. Is someone holding your **LADDER**?

2. What kind of **PERSON** is holding your ladder?

    A. Do you have to constantly **REMIND** them?

    B. Are they **CASUAL** or intentional?

    C. Do they have their eye on **YOU** or are they looking around?

    D. Do they have a firm grip on your "ladder" or **VISION**?

3. Qualities of an effective ladder holder

    A. **STRONG**

    B. **ATTENTIVE**

    C. **FAITHFUL**

    D. **FIRM**

    D. **LOYAL**

4. Ladder holders must be **TRAINED.**

    A. Very few ministers have **QUALIFIED** and **TRAINED** ladder holders.

    B. Your armor bearer/ **ASSISTANT** may not necessarily be your ladder holder.

    C. People need **CLEAR** instruction.

5. Ladder **POSITION** and perspective

    A. The greatest tragedy is to climb to the top of the ladder, only to find your ladder is leaning against the **WRONG** building.

    B. Assess

        (1) Where you want to go.

        (2) WHY you're on the ladder.

        (3) WHAT tools you need up there—you can't keep going up and down.

6. Two basic categories of ladder holders

    A. **LEADERS**

    B. **MANAGERS**

LEADERS	MANAGERS
Conceptualize outcome by working from the **FUTURE** back to the **PRESENT**.	Conceptualize plans by working from the **PAST** to the **PRESENT**.
Embrace a **MACRO** perspective —big picture	Embrace a **MICRO** perspective —snapshot
Favor **INNOVATIVE** thinking	Favor **ROUTINE** thinking
REVOLUTIONARY flair	**PROTECTOR** of the status quo
Emphasis on the **WHAT** and **WHY**	Emphasis on the **HOW** and **WHEN**
INSPIRING and motivating	**CONTROLLING** and directing
EXCITED by change	**THREATENED** by change
Move **QUICKLY**	Move **SLOWLY**
Identify **OPPORTUNITIES**	Identify **OBSTACLES**
Take **RISKS**	Avoid **RISKS**
Pursue acquisition of **RESOURCES**	Actions limited by **AVAILABLE** resources
PEOPLE centered	**SYSTEM** centered
IDEA centered	**PLAN** centered
People's approval is a **WANT**	People's approval is a **NEED**

APPENDIX

SUMMARY:
Managers get the most out of **THEMSELVES**. Leaders get the most out of **OTHERS**.

7. Turning ladder **HOLDERS** into ladder **CLIMBERS**

    A.   **SPIRITUAL** formation

        (1) Security issues

        (2) Finding purpose and destiny

    B.   **SKILL** formation

        (1) Helping other ladder holders

        (2) Delegation

        (3) Communication

    C.   **STRATEGIC** formation

        (1) Plan for developing other ladder holders

        (2) Mentoring—See it (**KNOW**); pursue it (**GROW**) and help others see it (**SHOW**)

        (3) Empowering others

8. Whose ladder are **YOU** holding?

    A.   In leadership you will always need **LADDER** holders.

B. In leadership you will always hold someone else's
    LADDER.

CONCLUSION:

IN LEADERSHIP, THE MOST IMPORTANT DECISION YOU
WILL MAKE IS SELECTING YOUR LADDER HOLDERS.

Notes

CHAPTER THREE
1.   March 19, 2001, p.2A.

CHAPTER FOUR
2.   *Futuring: Leading Your Church into Tomorrow* by Samuel R. Chand and Cecil Murphey (Grand Rapids, MI: Baker Books, 2002).
3.   Ibid.

CHAPTER FIVE
4.   p.8.
5.   Ibid.
6.   p.A12.

CHAPTER SEVEN
7.   March-April 2002, p.34.
8.   Ibid.
9.   An interview by Andrew Dietz in Catalystmagazine.com, p.18.
10. Ibid.
11. Ibid, p.20.
12. *Leader*, vol. 35, no. 1, p.126.
13. *Atlanta Journal-Constitution*, April 7, 2002, p.C1.
14. January 5, 2003, p.C1.
15. "Radio Shack's Leonard Roberts" by Lisa E. Davis, Sep. 2000, p.44.
16. Ibid.
17. "Beyond Greatness" by Mark Seal, *Celebrated Living*, Winter 2002, p.32.
18. *Leader*, vol. 26, no. 1, p.41.
19. Ibid.

CHAPTER EIGHT
20. Geoffrey W. Bromiley, *Theological Dictionary of the New Testament*, Abridged, Eerdmans, 1985, p.707.

OTHER HELPFUL RESOURCES
AVAILABLE FROM SAMUEL R. CHAND:

CONTACT:
SAMUEL R. CHAND MINISTRIES
P.O. Box 18145
Atlanta, GA 30316
1-888-777-2422 (toll free—ask for Erick Moon)
erick.moon@beulah.org
www.samchand.com (to e-purchase)

BOOKS

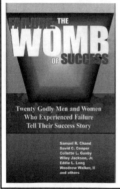

FAILURE:
the WOMB of SUCCESS

This book includes 20 great men and women who lived through failure. These include Bishop Eddie Long, Dr. Cynthia Hale, Dr. Wiley Jackson, Bishop Dale Bronner, Pastor Colette Gunby, Dr. Samuel Chand and others.

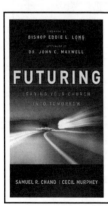

FUTURING:
Leading your Church into Tomorrow

The future has already happened. Learn about future-based leadership rooted in timeless biblical principals.

AUDIO

CREATING A
LEADERSHIP CULTURE

UNDERSTANDING
CONFLICTS:

Managing People in Your Life

FUTURING:

Leading your Church into
Tomorrow

CHANGE:

Leading Change Effectively

AUDIO

SRC MODEL OF LEADERSHIP:
- Skills
- Responsibilities
- Capabilities

FORMATION OF A LEADER:
- Spiritual
- Skill
- Strategic

PARADOXICAL LEADERSHIP

WHO'S HOLDING YOUR LADDER

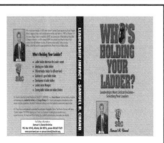